# The Ephesian Connection

*by*
*Donald Rumble*

**Destiny Image Publishers**
**P.O. Box 351**
**Shippensburg, PA 17257**

**"Speaking to the Purposes of God for this Generation"**

ISBN 1-56043-016-8

For Worldwide Distribution
Printed in the U.S.A.

# Dedication

I dedicate this book to our glorious Lord Jesus Christ and to His people. May He be glorified and may we become more committed to His centrality in our midst.

# Appreciation

I gratefully acknowledge the saints in my life who stood behind me in prayer as this book was taking shape. I am especially thankful for the brethren in Fountain of Life and the Saugerties Christian Fellowship, in the Kingston, Saugerties, N.Y. area. It was here that the Lord brought me back to Himself in 1971 and called me to minister His word. This company of people will always be my spiritual family, my roots.

Much thanks must go to my Dad for all his theological, editorial and fatherly advice. Without his input and encouragement I am sure I would have given up. Special thanks go to Vera Bixler for all her hours of editorial input and to Diana Morris for her contribution in proofreading. This project would not have the grammatical clarity that it does without them. Much appreciation also goes to Lois Quad, Wayne Veino and Arthur Butt for their work on the computer to make this manuscript camera ready. Finally, there is my Mom, whose love, input, sense of humor and intercessions for my life have contributed far more than I can express.

# Contents

# Foreword

When you have just finished reading a book you would like your friends to enjoy, you are somewhat limited. You can either buy books for them, or hope to find a way to encourage them to get their own. Today I can almost transcend those usual limitations. I am privileged and delighted, by writing this foreword to make the widest possible recommendation of this book.

Most avid readers are aware that Paul's letter to the Ephesians has already been handled by many scholars, and some of their writings are most helpful. In view of this I must confess I first approached this book with a bit of apprehension.

I wondered!

Could another book really add much? Could this author possibly have some insights which had escaped the attention of godly men—who are skilled in the message of Ephesians? Could he catch and express what I have considered to be the imperative and ultimate truths of the apostle Paul's heart?

I am amazed!

Indeed, the Holy Spirit has guided the author in unfolding some very precious insights—all from the twenty-three verses in the first chapter of Ephesians. As you read, you will recognize a new richness and depth in the significant phrases which the apostle Paul uses. Indeed, I predict many will come alive!

In this hour when man-centeredness prevails, I am most grateful for this truly God-centered emphasis which encourages us to see all things from God's viewpoint—to see the glorious unveiling of his Father-heart and His purpose for His Son and many sons.

May I urge you to read with a "bended knee" and a seeking heart. Fully expect to hear God speak. Don't rush through! Hold these Pauline phrases of truth before the Lord, asking Him to reveal each one more fully so as to establish your own walk in helping fulfill His eternal purpose.

DeVern Fromke

# Introduction

In the summer of 1985, after a rather trying year of intense traveling ministry, I decided I needed to stay home for awhile. I was not sure exactly how God wanted me to focus my time, but I knew He had something in store for me. One evening, as a friend and I were having an ice cream at Friendly's, another friend who was employed by the local Christian radio station walked in. The conversation soon turned to how the folks at the station were looking for local ministers to teach over the air. My first reaction was somewhat reserved since I had never done it before or ever considered that it should become a major part of my ministry. However, over the next couple of weeks, the thought would not go away. Then the Lord began to speak to me out of Paul's epistle to the Ephesians. As I studied, He indicated that I was to share over the radio the insights He was giving me. Interestingly enough, I did not sense that the program was to be primarily for bringing new people into our local church, but simply to be a blessing for whoever the Lord had listening. Little did I know that His main intention was to have me take my extensive notes from the sessions and use them as the basis of this book! Over a period of forty-three weeks, God opened up the First chapter of Ephesians in a way I had never seen before. The result is not a treatise of exhaustive research, but a compilation of insights coming from times with the Lord as we met around the contents of this chapter.

As I meditated and prayed, it seemed that what God wanted to accomplish through the book was to give prophetic comment on the Scripture and draw the reader more into communion with Him. Therefore, I am presenting in thirty-one chapters what the Lord revealed, one for each day of the month. Each chapter stands as a unit complete in itself and yet each contributes to the whole picture of what Paul was saying. Hopefully, this approach will encourage those who read to have both a consistent time of communion with the Lord and a consistent time of meditation on His word.

Paul's letter to the Ephesians is filled with much significant truth concerning God's eternal purpose. This truth did not come to him before he met the Lord. It came first as the result of a confrontation with Jesus on the road to Damascus and then by divine revelation as he walked with Him. When he bowed his knee to Christ, a "connection" was made. Then as Paul lived and walked in intimate communion with Him, God gave him insight that would affect the lives of millions of people. The "Ephesian connection," the intimate communion that Paul had with God that gave birth to this epistle, indicates the call on each of us to respond to the Lord's presence.

In the final analysis, it will not be those who intellectually know the Bible well who will have the greatest insight and reward, but those who spend time with its Author. They will not only have an intimacy with Him (which is the greatest reward of all), they will also receive insight into His perspective concerning what He has written. Those who respond to God's primary call on their lives and walk intimately with Him will find that their evangelizing, preaching and church building reflect God's authority more than man's ingenuity. The plans and programs of men have not sufficed in building His Church, nor in bringing God's authority to bear on the nations. The world has seen the best that the Church has to offer and is not impressed. What is needed now is for us to return to our first love and find our true identity in His presence. Then His plan for us and the nations will become clear. How can we expect the world to respond to God's authority when the Church does her own thing in His name and then seeks His blessing? Come let us return to the Lord. Let us hear what He would say and let us go forth in His name, effecting His plan in our generation.

# Chapter 1

# Paul, an Apostle of Jesus Christ

"Paul, an apostle of Christ Jesus by the will of God, to the saints who are at Ephesus, and who are faithful in Christ Jesus..." (Eph. 1:1)

Apostle. When we hear this word, we usually think of men in the New Testament who wrote the Scriptures, did mighty miracles, walked in intimacy with Jesus and established new churches. While all of this is applicable, the word "apostle" simply means "a sent one," one known primarily for the fact he has been sent by another. An apostle's main function is to *accurately represent* the One who sent him. The first person one usually thinks of in connection with this ministry is Paul. However, the premier example of apostleship is Jesus Christ (Heb. 3:1).

Jesus did not come from heaven on His own initiative; the Father *sent* Him. Thus His primary ministry on the earth was to do His Father's will and represent Him accurately.

"...the Son can do nothing of Himself, unless it is
something He sees the Father doing; for whatever the Father
does, these things the Son also does in like manner"
(Jn. 5:19)

Jesus was able to say:

"...I always do the things that are pleasing to Him... "
(Jn. 8:29)

Consequently...

"...He who has seen Me has seen the Father..." (Jn. 14:9)

Jesus was the perfect representative. Just as Jesus expressed the Father, so Paul was called by grace to reveal the
Lord Jesus. Paul saw himself as a representative of Christ
everywhere he went.

Today, many represent religious institutions, schools of
doctrine, or methods of church order. But God is looking for
a people who will represent *Him*. This requires that such
men and women first come into His presence and know Him
in an intimate manner.

"...this is eternal life, that they may know Thee, the only
true God, and Jesus Christ whom Thou hast sent." (Jn.
17:3)

The word translated as "know" could also be translated,
"the intimate experiencing of another." We are called to
*know* the Lord, *to intimately experience Him.* He wants us to
come, stand in His presence and understand Him as He is.
Then as we go into the world on His behalf, we will not
only speak truth about Him (things we have heard or read),

we will also proclaim who He is and what is in His heart on the basis of face-to-face revelation.

God said to Moses...

"...come up in the morning to Mount Sinai, and present yourself there to Me on the top of the mountain." (Ex. 34:2)

In effect, He said, "Moses, come up and *be* there." In obedience, Moses went up and stood in the presence of the Lord. Out of that encounter came "nation altering" consequences. The course of Israel, the way that men worshiped God and even the history of mankind took a new direction, because of that meeting between Moses and God. Significant insights concerning the purposes of God and the building of His house were given. They are still valid for the building of His *spiritual* house in our generation! What tremendous repercussions! All this because a man responded to the call to stand in the presence of the Lord.

Today there is so much religious activity, that it is easy to get caught up in the things of God, more than with God Himself. However, God's call is that His people would take time to sit before Him, to intimately experience Him and come to know Him as He really is. Only there will we hear what He would say to us. Only then will we go forth with *His* words in our mouths. Only then will we accurately represent Him.

Though the church at Antioch stood with Paul, laid hands on him, agreed with his burden and call, and sent him out to fulfill the purposes of God, he never referred to himself as an apostle of Antioch. Paul was an apostle of *Jesus,* called to represent *Him.* Nor did he ever attempt to export "Antioch-ism", i.e., he did not seek to establish little corporate "clones" of what had happened at Antioch in the places he ministered. He was not interested in duplicating elsewhere the experience of the saints in his "home church." Rather, he endeavored to move spontaneously in the life of the Lord Jesus, so that God could raise up *diverse and varied corporate expressions of His life.* Obviously there were similarities, such as the establishing of elders and deacons in each local church. However, each group was made up of unique people with unique personalities, callings and ministries. Thus, Paul desired to see fellowships reflecting that diversity raised up around the life of the Lord Jesus wherever the gospel was received.

The key to understanding Paul's method of ministry is this: he wanted *Jesus revealed.* He was not in love with a doctrine or a way of doing things. He was in love with a person, and he wanted Him to be central and magnified in the Church.

It was not always so for him. He says of his former life:

"...I used to persecute the church of God beyond measure, and tried to destroy it; and I was advancing in Judaism beyond many of my contemporaries among my countrymen." (Gal. 1:13,14)

While "moving up the ranks" in Jewish religion, Paul actually persecuted and strove against God! He cast Christians into prison, trying to force them to blaspheme, and all the time believing he was rendering service to God (Acts 26:2-11). He saw the Christian phenomenon as a kind of "infection" in Judaism that needed to be eradicated.

However, one day on the road to Damascus, while fuming in his fanatical zeal against the Christians, Paul met the fulfillment of all he had studied. He had sat at the feet of a man named Gamaliel and gained much knowledge of the Law and the Prophets. The thrust of Old Testament theology was that one day there would come One who would be the Redeemer of God's people. Paul read the Scriptures and thought he understood them. But on that fateful day when he met Him, the fulfillment of it all, as he looked at this One whom he had studied, he realized there was no comparison between mere knowledge and the actual person of the Lord Jesus Christ. As he saw Him, he fell on his face and his life was never the same.

From that time on, *the glory of Christ* became his message. Paul wanted to see the person of *Jesus Himself* revealed through his preaching. He simply sought to become the bond-slave of his Messiah, even unto prison and death. No wonder he made such an impact in his lifetime upon secular and religious institutions. He was not sharing a philosophy or a method of Christian ministry. He was revealing a person. Even as Jesus had come to reveal the Father, so Paul saw that his calling was to reveal the person of Christ.

If we would see Christ revealed in our personal lives and ministries, we must return to a first love relationship where we can intimately experience Him. When we sit in His presence, knowing Him and hearing His voice, we will be enabled to go into the world as an apostolic people, accurately representing the One who has sent us.

# Chapter 2

# To the Saints
# Who Are at Ephesus

"Paul, an apostle of Christ Jesus by the will of God, to the saints who are at Ephesus, and who are faithful in Christ Jesus: Grace to you and peace from God our Father and the Lord Jesus Christ." (Eph. 1:1,2)

One of the first things to strike us in this verse is the singular nature of the house of the Lord. The saints in Ephesus all belonged to the same church! Today, there is only one Church in all the earth, but she is divided. God's view of His house differs from that of men. We may see many churches in an area, He sees but one. God wants us to catch His perspective, rather than simply look around and accept the obvious as normal. What God considers as normal, differs from what men deem as normal. The best of our humanity is subnormal in God's eyes.

"...all have sinned and fall short of the glory of God..." (Rom. 3:23)

Even those of us born of the Spirit fall short of God's glory. It does not say all have sinned and *fell* short only when they were unbelievers, but rather that all have sinned and *presently fall short* of the glory of God. In ourselves, we are subnormal. The only normal man who ever walked on the face of the earth was Jesus! He totally fulfilled everything He came to accomplish. He never sinned. He never came short of the glory of God. But every other individual has sinned and continues to fall short of His glory. Because of this, *our viewpoint also falls short of the Lord's perspective.* In order to see as God sees, to understand the way things really are, we need to have His prophetic anointing upon us. Furthermore, He *wants* us to see as He sees. He wants us to view the lost and the condition of His Church as He does. He wants us to observe our world and His actions in it through His eyes, not through the eyes of the news media, the educational system, the entertainment industry, etc.

There is One who reigns over the kingdoms of men who is uniquely involved with each life. His name is Jesus. He is King of Kings and Lord of Lords! He looks down into the hearts of men and into the course of nations, and He fully apprehends what actually is unfolding. What truly matters is His perspective, not ours. His viewpoint is infallible. What we read about or think within ourselves is not the final word or a total picture. Only His judgment is complete and perfect.

However, when we compare the Church in its present condition with God's description in the Bible of how it ought to be, the two do not match. The Church today does not appear as a glorious house, a people separated from the world, as pictured in Scripture, but one that is divided and badly tarnished. If we had gone to the city of Ephesus, we would have found a single united Church. This does not necessarily imply they all met in the same building. In some of the larger cities, there were too many believers for that to be possible. The logistics were against it. But in each city, the Body of Christ was unified. Christians were marked by their love for one another, not by sectarianism. Men of God were not off by themselves building their own separate ministries and followings. In every place where valid apostolic ministries had laid foundations, the Church was a singular people served by leadership that sought to stand together under the headship of the Lord Jesus.

Jesus prayed that there would be a people in the earth moving in the same kind of oneness that He had with His Father.

"...that they may be perfected in unity [lit. into a unit], that the world may know that Thou didst send Me..." (Jn. 17:23)

There will come a uniting of God's people upon the earth! Jesus prayed for it, and that prayer will be answered! This unity will be so obvious, the world will look and declare that truly Jesus was sent from the Father. It will be "fleshed out" in life-styles having such practical implications that even those not born of the Spirit and without discernment will be able to recognize it. Mankind will be without excuse. But today such unity is not in evidence. In city after city, the Church has fallen short of that which Jesus intends to bring forth. Therefore we must not be complacent! We must see where God wants to take us and submit to His plan to bring us there! We as a people, must not settle back, become comfortable and think that where we are is good enough. God wants to take us beyond our present experience. He desires to establish the one house of His body in every place.

In local fellowships, we must not compete with other churches in our cities. We must not attempt to take people from other gatherings of God's children in order that they might join us. Our burden must be to give ourselves to serve them. Each local fellowship must face this question: How can we serve God's people in our area? As we abide in the Lord Jesus, in our individual circumstances, in the particular local church He has placed us in, and serve those around us as led by the Spirit, then *God will unify His people!* Our best efforts will not produce what Jesus prayed for. You cannot organize the miraculous nor can you legislate unity! Unity of the faith will not come from debating on doctrine. Unity will come when God's people return to their first love. Whenever we focus on a love relationship with Christ, we always find others standing alongside us who love Him as well. They may not be people we would have chosen, but their love for Him has brought us together! We may even find alongside us those who will disagree with us on various points of doctrine. Then we will find Jesus saying to us, "If you love Me, love those I love!" Our response may be, "But Lord, we don't see eye to eye." But His word to us will be, "I died for them. Receive them as I have received you. I will change them and I will also change you."

Whenever people make Jesus their first love, they inevitably find Him bringing others who love Him into their lives. He said He would build His Church. Today He is bringing believers together from diverse backgrounds with different giftings, ministries and personalities. It is only as we are filled with the Holy Spirit and maintain an attitude of brokenness and humility that we can jointly walk together in true spiritual unity. The greatest cause of division in the Church is not different doctrines, but unbroken men and women. We are used to running our own lives. We like to do things a certain way. Then when we see others who function differently, we feel free just to walk away from them. But God wants to make us into broken, humble servants. *"Incompatibility" is not a basis for division.* God was very "incompatible" with the world; yet He sent His Son to die on its behalf! Consider how different the Lord Jesus was from the world He came to 2000 years ago. It was undoubtedly offensive to His holy character. Yet He gave Himself even to the shedding of His blood for the forgiveness of our sins. In His ministry, He loved and spoke truth to those who were the outcasts of society. He was the perfect servant. If we would contribute to the unity of God's house, we must become servants conformed to the character of the Lord Jesus. If we do not, we will misrepresent Him even when we speak His truth. We can speak His truth and destroy with it, or we can speak His truth and build with it. *Unbroken men often destroy with the same truth that broken men build with.* Unbroken men have damaged and divided the Church down through history.

In the past, God has allowed men to build little "Christian empires" and sects around various doctrines and personalities. But in these days, God requires that His people be broken and humbled in His presence as a prerequisite to being a part of His great work in uniting the Church. He is gathering a people *unto Himself.* As we come to Him we will discover others who love Him even as we do. There we will find the Lord requiring us to "wash the feet" of those around us with love and truth.

When Jesus washed the disciples' feet with natural water in the thirteenth Chapter of John, it was simply an extension of what He had been doing for three years with the spiritual water of God's word! He had served them with the truth. Often they had not understood what He was saying, so He had patiently taken time to explain the Kingdom of God to them. Thus, we need to walk in the same manner as we minister God's truth in our generation. We are servants of the Lord and servants of His people. Jesus said:

"...the greatest among you shall be your servant." (Matt. 23:11)

Today He challenges us to become the least, to become as a child, to be a slave. This is where true greatness is found. We must not seek recognition or our "name in lights." Rather, we must seek how we can be poured out so others can come into all that God has purposed for them. This is the objective of all true ministry. Leadership is called to equip the saints for the work of service. We are not called to simply have our own ministry. Therefore let us seek to be poured out in service on behalf of those God has placed in our lives. Let there be no striving for position or running after fame. Let us only run after Him! For in so doing, unity in the Lord's house will be attained.

# Chapter 3

# He Has Blessed Us Just as He Chose Us

"Blessed be the God and Father of our Lord Jesus Christ, who *has blessed us* with every spiritual blessing in the heavenly places in Christ, *just as He chose us* in Him before the foundation of the world." (Eph. 1:3,4, emphasis mine)

Happy is the man whom God chooses and brings near to dwell in His house (Ps. 65:4, paraphrased). Without God's choosing, man cannot have a right relationship with his Creator. Thus, it is indeed good to rejoice over His choice of us. But we need to recognize that there is far more. Paul says we have been *blessed* just as we have been chosen! We can be God's chosen people and yet not appropriate the blessing that is our inheritance. If we do not see the fullness of what Christ purchased for us through His death and resurrection, we will live and minister at a level far below what we ought to. We need to understand the dimension of the Spirit that God intends for us to live and move in.

If He has blessed us *just as* He has chosen us, this raises some interesting questions. How were we chosen? Was it because we were worthy? Was it through our holiness or sinless lives? Obviously not. It was based solely on the mercy and grace of God. There was no holiness or righteousness in anyone to make such a one attractive to Him. He took the initiative and reached toward us before we even knew He existed. We did not strive to be chosen, and we did not earn it. Thankfulness fills our hearts as we see this truth. Worship flows forth from our lives when we understand who God is and what He has done for us. If then our participation in being chosen was through His initiative and not our efforts, then it follows that we inherit the blessings the same way! There is a realm of the Spirit open to us which is not attained by striving, human effort, or human ingenuity. It is a dimension of heavenly life that God calls us to, and *we enter by believing in Him!*

"Blessed be the God and Father of our Lord Jesus Christ, who has blessed us with every spiritual blessing *in the heavenly places* in Christ..." (Eph. 1:3, emphasis mine)

My first thought on reading this verse was, "Well, who needs spiritual blessings in heavenly places? I need blessings in earthly places! This is where I am living. This is where I have problems with people, both in the Church and in the world. This is where the conflicts are. So what do I need blessings up there for?" But Paul is trying to get us to see another realm. In Ephesians 2:6, he tells us that God has...

"...seated us with Him in the heavenly places, in Christ Jesus."

In reality, we are already seated in the heavenlies! We are called to live in a higher realm than the unsaved. We are to be a prophetic people, *a people of the heavenlies while standing on the earth, a people who have "made the connection,"* tapping the power of the ages to come! We need to take the focus off what is temporal, what can be seen and touched, and learn to see the unseen and live there. A man of faith does not live according to what can be seen, but according to what cannot be seen. Our inheritance as God's people will not be appropriated by human ingenuity or strength.

Nonetheless, though we do not have to strive for God's blessings, we often fail to attain them. Why? Because of our lack of vision.

"Where there is no vision, the people are unrestrained." (Prov. 29:18)

For example, a runner in a track meet has the goal line set before him, and he runs toward it with all of his strength. You won't see him wandering off the track to make conversation with the spectators. Nor does he get distracted by some pretty flowers and stop to smell them along the way. His goal restrains him. He presses forward with all of his might, not at liberty to respond to whatever urges suddenly come to mind. The vision holds him in check.

The question we face is this. What do we see set in front of us? What goal? What mark? What prize? What has so captured our attention that we are restrained in our lives?

Why is it that we cannot get away with certain activities and attitudes this year that we got away with last year? What has so captured our vision that we are "hemmed in" by a new life-style? Is it not because we have seen Him? The greatest gift God could give us is Himself. What could be added to Him? In what way is He incomplete? Is it not true that in Him are found all the treasures of wisdom and knowledge? Is it not true that the wealth of heaven resides in this One, the Lord Jesus? If anything else fills our vision, it is an idol, be it ministry, wealth, a desire for recognition or power.

In the world, we see men's lives constrained by purpose. If one decides he is going to be a millionaire by the age of 40, he will make extraordinary sacrifices to fill his coffer. Or if he has political ambitions, he counts the cost and considers what it will entail to attain the desired office. He "hems in his life" because of the vision he has for his future. With a sense of total abandon, he throws himself into the process of seeing the vision fulfilled. Has Jesus captured your attention and filled your vision?

Jesus said,

"He who loves father or mother more than *Me* is not worthy of Me; and he who loves son or daughter more than *Me* is not worthy of Me." (Matt. 10:37, emphasis mine)

The whole object of life is *Jesus Himself!* Why did He present Himself as the focus and objective of mankind? Was He trying to keep us from enjoying a rich and fulfilling life? No. On the contrary, those who pursue any goal other than Him will never know true fulfillment. They will never understand real peace or come to grips with the meaning of life.

But those who have found Him, have *life itself!* Jesus is God's greatest gift to mankind. Neither heaven nor earth has anything better to offer!

What is your present need? Is it for peace? Behold the Prince of Peace. Do you need insight? Consider Christ, the wisdom of God. Or is your need for healing? There is Christ, the power of God. Do you need righteousness? The Scriptures say He is made unto us righteousness (1 Cor. 1:30). Everything that heaven has to offer men is found in this One, the Lord Jesus. He is our inheritance!

In Philippians 3:7,8, Paul writes these words.

> "But whatever things were gain to me; those things I have counted as loss for the sake of *Christ.* More than that, I count all things to be loss in view of the surpassing value of *knowing Christ Jesus* my Lord, *for whom* I have suffered the loss of all things, and count them but rubbish in order that I may *gain Christ."* (emphasis mine)

Paul possessed a great desire and longing for the person of the Lord Jesus. Even as men desire to gain their inheritance, so Paul sought to gain Him. It cost Paul everything; it will cost us no less. The question we must ask ourselves is this: Is He worth it? Heaven says He is. What does our lifestyle say?

Let us arise and live in our inheritance. Let us abide in Him. As we do, we along with Paul will find that God...

> "...has blessed us with *every* spiritual blessing in the heavenly places *in Christ."* (Eph. 1:3, emphasis mine)

# Chapter 4

# Before the Foundation
# of the World

"...just as He chose us in Him before the foundation of
the world, that we should be holy and blameless before
Him." (Eph. 1:4)

How was it possible for God to choose men before they
existed? How could He choose people for His purpose, even
before He created the planet upon which they would live? In
order to understand how, we must be aware that God is not
bound by time. He has an eternal perspective. From eternity,
He could view His whole plan from beginning to end. He
saw the fall of Adam, with the resulting consequence of darkness and sin spreading to His creation. He foresaw His incarnation and bearing the sins of mankind through His death
on the cross. Thus, from eternity, He understood the awesome
price He would have to pay to redeem men. But, He also
saw the joy awaiting Him in His ultimate resurrection as
victor over sin, death and Hell. He saw it all! Adam's fall

and the ensuing problems did not take God by surprise. It was all included in calculating the cost to prepare a bride for Himself!

"...who for the joy set before Him endured the cross, despising the shame, and has sat down at the right hand of the throne of God." (Heb. 12:2)

In viewing that bridal company, He regarded each of us as individuals. He loved each of us and when He came to purchase us, He came gladly.

Many Christians have nagging doubts about God's call on their lives. They acknowledge their salvation and accept forgiveness of their sins. But there is no *confidence* in His call. This is evidenced by their continual focus on failures and how worthless they feel to the Lord. However, the call of God for each of us existed before we did anything right or wrong! It is not based on what we have done in this age; it is based on grace granted to us from eternity. From eternity He saw us, loved us and called us unto Himself. We have been loved a long, long time! He foreknew each of us *including our weaknesses* and, in His call, has extended all the grace we will ever need (2 Tim. 1:9).

"But God demonstrates His own love toward us, in that while we were yet sinners, Christ died for us." (Rom. 5:6)

God's heart was already set upon us with thoughts of love, before we even thought of Him, before we even considered whether there was a God! In Ephesians 3:17, Paul states we need to be "rooted and grounded" in that love, in

His heart of love for us. This is the foundation of our faith; not doctrine, but a living person!

"For no man can lay a foundation other than the one which is laid, which is Jesus Christ." (1 Cor. 3:11)

We are to be built upon this One who is love personified. As we are "rooted and grounded" in Him, we will be securely founded in our Christian walk. A believer is only as strong as he is rightly related to the foundation of his faith. The Rock (Christ Himself) is solid and firmly placed. The issue then is, how adequately are we related to Him? Do we believe in Him as we ought to? Do we wholly trust Him and respond with a heart of love?

"Behold I am laying in Zion a stone, a tested stone, a costly cornerstone for the foundation, firmly placed. He who believes in it will not be disturbed [lit. in a hurry]." (Isa. 28:16)

One characteristic that marks our society, even Christian circles, is that we are people in a hurry. Many rush here and there with much to do and many places to go. Great activity motivated by a "hurried" spirit reflects a lack of peace in the hearts of men. Obviously, there are valid things that need to be accomplished. But if we believe in Jesus as we should, our lives will not be marked by hurriedness, frustration, anxiety or panic, for we will be at rest in Him.

God is not rushed or in a hurry. He has not fallen behind schedule in His purposes. He is not nervously pacing "the corridors of heaven" wondering how human need grew so great! He is not amazed that so many people are still unsaved at this point in history. The proliferation of cults and false prophets has not taken Him by surprise. His course of action planned for the coming years will not be in reaction to events that catch Him unawares. This is not to imply God does not care about such things. He is deeply concerned about sin, deception and human frailties. But heaven is characterized by peace, not anxiety, for God foreknows those who will respond to His call. He foreknows the end of it all.

"And we know that God causes all things to work together for good to those who love God, to those who are called according to His purpose. For whom He foreknew, He also predestined to become conformed to the image of His Son, that He might be the first-born among many brethren." (Rom. 8:28,29)

We all remember when we started late for some scheduled event and had to hurry to arrive on time. But God started His "program" early enough so that He would never be rushed. He began "before the foundation of the world." From eternity, God saw clearly the men and amount of time and grace that would be needed to fulfill His purposes, both in individual lives as well as in the maturing of the Church. He is not running short on either. There is not a grace shortage in heaven. Neither is there an uneasy sense of panic. Peace reigns.

God is not a servant to time, it serves Him!

"...in these last days has spoken to us in His Son, whom He appointed heir of all things, through whom also He made the world [lit. ages]." (Heb. 1:2)

"Now to the King eternal, [lit. of the ages]." (1 Tim. 1:17)

God created the ages of time for His purpose, and today His plan is being fulfilled within that framework. Therefore, His call on our lives is not based on what we have done in this age, but on Him and His eternal perspective. Thus, like Him, we are not to be rushed in our spirits as we seek to serve Him. When we believe in Him, knowing that He is actively involved in our lives and circumstances and that He is moving according to a plan designed in eternity, we refuse to be rushed! We retain concern for the needs we see around us (unsaved friends and loved ones, sickness, deception, etc.), but we serve with a sense of rest and confidence in His call on our lives! Peace prevails in our hearts, because we believe in an active, sovereign God who has chosen us.

We are called to minister peace in the earth. Multitudes demonstrate for peace in society. "Stop war," they cry. But the peace of God is not like that of the world.

"Peace I leave with you; My peace I give to you; *not as the world gives,* do I give to you." (Jn. 14:27, emphasis mine)

The world's peace is the absence of conflict; God's peace is His presence with us in the *midst* of conflict! In Jesus' earthly ministry, He clashed with the religious leaders of His day. The same was true of the apostle Paul. Yet they ministered the peace of God. Our objective then is not to avoid conflict, but rather to "lay hold" of God's presence and power when conflict inevitably arises. To follow Christ is to oppose the powers of darkness. Opposition then should not surprise us. When we believe in Him as we ought to, we will be able to minister His peace to others, even while in the turmoil! God desires to bring His supernatural peace to us within the circumstances of our lives. Peace is to be experienced in the throes of shaking!

When we are not rightly related to Him, we will be characterized by anxiety, frustration, panic and a rushed spirit as conflict or turmoil arises. Frustration can turn to anger. Anger either gets vented on others or suppressed, resulting in ulcers or any number of illnesses. The lack of peace is either externalized or internalized. Either way, the Kingdom of God is not being expressed as it should be. Anger can then lead to despair. We find ourselves thinking, "This situation will never change!" However...

"...the Kingdom of God is...righteousness and peace and joy in the Holy Spirit." (Rom. 14:17)

Consider this question: "Would you seek counsel concerning the peace of God from someone who was nervously pacing back and forth in the room as he talked?" Do you think his counsel would have much impact on your life? My point is this. We undermine the message of the Kingdom of God if we are not at rest. We are called to minister the Prince of Peace to others. When we see all that needs to be done in the Church, all who need salvation, and all our personal pressing needs, if we do not have internal peace, our lives will conflict with the message we preach! To be effective, we must have confidence in our eternal roots in Christ and His call on our lives. We must believe in the Lord being active in our lives today. The result will be both peace in our hearts and His kingdom expressed through us.

"...who has saved us, and called us with a holy calling, not according to our works, but according to His own purpose and grace which was granted us in Christ Jesus from all eternity." (2 Tim. 1:9)

# Chapter 5

# Holy and Blameless Before Him

"...just as He chose us in Him before the foundation of the world, that we should be holy and blameless before Him." (Eph. 1:4)

God has chosen us to be a people who walk holy and blameless *before Him*. However, we tend to focus on whether we appear to be holy and blameless *before men*. What others think of us is often very important to us. We want to be esteemed. In fact, we are taught that we *need* to be esteemed. Thus we buy into the old cliches of "putting our best foot forward" and presenting ourselves in the "best light possible." Jesus, on the other hand, never concerned Himself with whether or not He made a good impression on people. Of course, neither did He endeavor to make a bad one; He simply sought to please His Father. His life and ministry were not governed by what men thought of Him, but by the will of Him who sent Him.

The most devastating result of being a man-pleaser is to appear holy before others and yet be a failure in God's sight.

He sees in us what others cannot see. He knows the attitudes and motives of our hearts, of which those around us are unaware. God desires truth in the inward parts (Ps. 51:6). He has called us to walk in honesty before Him. When we pray, we must communicate our true feelings, speaking to Him of our frustrations and disappointments as well as our victories. God is impressed with reality, not artificiality. We should not just "say prayers" in His direction, but commune with Him. He is someone with whom we can be open. How foolish to try to hide from Him. Yet how much more foolish to try to impress Him with pious words, words that do not truly express our hearts! Such words may appear holy to others, but God seeks reality. People around us may be impressed. He is not! As a matter of fact, *He is not impressed with what impresses men, and He is impressed with what men often think is unimportant.* His value system differs from ours. He wants us to learn His ways rather than to take our ways and attribute them to Him. Therein lies a significant difference between Christianity and religion.

Christianity is to be marked by relationship between God and His people. Religion, on the other hand, is marked by men endeavoring to impose on God and others what they determine to be relevant. In some Christian assemblies, it does not matter what God wants to say or do in a gathering, because men have already decided what they intend to accomplish. While what occurs may seem to bless men, the question that should be answered is whether God is blessed or not! *What impresses God will ultimately impact men; what impresses men will ultimately impact no one!*

Throughout history, the Church has sought the admiration of the world. She has taken things the world has deemed important and given them significance in her midst, even though God never indicated that they were important to Him (e.g., education, buildings, types of dress, etc.). As a result, when unbelievers look at the Church, they assume that what they observe reflects God's priorities. However, we have misrepresented the Lord. Thus, our impact on society has been blunted.

> "In the same way, you wives, be submissive to your own husbands so that even if any of them are disobedient to the word, they may be won without a word by the behavior of their wives, as they observe your chaste and respectful behavior. And let not your adornment be merely external—braiding the hair, and wearing gold jewelry, or putting on dresses, but let it be the hidden person of the heart, with the imperishable quality of a gentle and quiet spirit, which is precious in the sight of God." (1 Pet. 3:1-4)

The thrust of this passage deals with how saved women can influence their unsaved husbands for the sake of the Kingdom of God. A key word Peter uses is "adornment." Adornment means "to beautify." He instructs women not to put an emphasis on external adornment. True beautifying is an *internal* more than an external process and yields a comeliness precious in God's sight. Peter's instruction is that if Christian women want to win their unsaved husbands, they should *not* primarily seek to attract their husbands to *themselves.* They should seek to become more attractive in the sight of *the Lord!* As they submit to His dealings in their hearts, His character will be formed more clearly in them.

The resulting beauty will then have a greater impact on their husbands than any external adornment they could ever devise! As they grow increasingly beautiful in God's sight, their impact on those around them also grows.

This is where the Church has most misunderstood God's strategy for evangelism. *We have sought to attract the world to ourselves, instead of seeking above all, to become more attractive in His sight.* We are first of all His bride, and secondarily we are ministers to the world. But what the world thinks of us has taken precedence in our eyes. Thus, we have adopted practices that, while not necessarily evil, are not God's priority. *As a result, the Church has been camouflaged instead of adorned!* When one is camouflaged, he is hidden from plain view. He accomplishes this by taking things from his surroundings and wearing them in order to mask his uniqueness in the setting. Yet it is precisely the Church's uniqueness in the world that must be maintained at all costs! Jesus is not coming back for a bride that "fits in," but for one that "stands out"! He longs for His people to come forth in *His* likeness. He is pouring out His grace upon us so that when we are properly adorned with character, He will come for us.

> "Let us rejoice and be glad and give the glory to Him, for the marriage of the Lamb has come and His bride has made herself ready...And it was given to her to clothe herself in fine linen, bright and clean; for the fine linen is the righteous acts of the saints. And I saw heaven opened; and behold, a white horse, and He who sat upon it is called Faithful and True." (Rev. 19:7,8,11)

Notice, the coming of the Lord is in direct response to the bride making herself ready. Notice too, that it is *given to her* (this emphasizes the grace of God) to *make herself* ready (this emphasizes human responsibility). She prepares for *Him*; she is His. Her focus is not on needs around her, but on Him. However, the fine linen she puts on are deeds of righteousness springing from her heart in behalf of the needy, *which indicate* her readiness for His coming. God is speaking to us, His people, to arise today in obedience and give ourselves in life-styles of serving and caring for the needs of those around us. For what we do in the horizontal dimension will reflect the reality of our vertical relationship with the Lord.

However, our first priority is not horizontal, but vertical. We are not primarily a people given to the world, but to Him! Our ministry to the world should exhibit that unique identity we have in Him! Many times Christian leaders use guilt manipulation on God's people by focusing on the ever-prevailing needs around them, in order to motivate the Church to action. But moral obligation is not the motivating force in the Church's ministry to the world; love is! The adornment of the Bride (our righteous acts) is put on for *His* sake! *He* is our focus and our goal. Our reaching out to the world is the by-product of the grace He lavishes upon us to prepare us as a Bride *for Him!* Guilt manipulation can generate activity, but it will never bring forth the Bride or bring back the Groom!

Let us shed the camouflage we have to put on to impress the world and let us walk with this one ambition: to be pleasing to Him.

# Chapter 6

# He Predestined Us to Adoption as Sons

Many Christians consider the gospel as something that only addresses the forgiveness of sins and the attainment of heaven. Certainly having our sins forgiven is the first step in the process of obtaining our inheritance; however, God's purposes are much greater.

"In love He predestined us to adoption as sons through Jesus Christ to Himself, according to the kind intention of His will." (Eph. 1:5)

God has predestined us to something called, "the adoption as sons" (HUIOTHESIA), which comes from two Greek words, HUIOS... sons and THESIS... placement. So HUIO-THESIA could also be translated as "the placement of sons." This term refers, in part, to sons stepping into their place in the family of God. It is not referring primarily to being born of the Spirit. When we are born again, we become children (TEKNON... a born one) of God.

"But as many as received Him, to them He gave the right to become children [TEKNON] of God." (Jn. 1:12)

To be born of the Spirit happens in a moment, but *placement as mature sons* may take years. If God's plan was simply to get us into heaven, then why did He not take us home the minute we believed? Then there would be no chance of backsliding! But neither would there be any opportunities to grow in the character of God and bear fruit in this life. Nor would we have the opportunity to extend the Kingdom of God in the earth. *The inheritance awaiting us has to do with this life, not just the one to come!*

"...you were sealed in Him with the Holy Spirit of promise, who is given as *a pledge of our inheritance."* (Eph. 1:13,14, emphasis mine)

Even as a down payment (e.g., in the purchase of a car) is the first part of what is to follow, so also the indwelling Holy Spirit is a beginning of the glories to come. In drinking of Him, we...

"have tasted...the powers of the age to come." (Heb. 6:5)

If we misunderstand the initial portion of the inheritance, we miss God's purpose for this life! Why has the Spirit of God been given to us? One reason is that He seeks to place us as mature sons in the family of God in order to enjoy fully the inheritance that is ours in *this life*. But we often settle for less than God's best.

One of satan's tactics is to convince us that faith in God only concerns the past or future. Some in the Church believe

God moved in great power and authority in the past (as seen in the book of Acts) and that He will again in the future (at Jesus' second coming), but that He is not doing very much in the present. Somehow Christians are simply to sit and wait faithfully for some coming time when the glory of God will again be manifested. Until then, we are expected to study the past as we wait for the future. This suggests that today we are supposedly in the midst of a great irrelevant "parenthesis" in which God only silently looks on. Nothing could be further from the truth! Jesus said,

> "I will not leave you as orphans; I will come to you." (Jn. 14:18)

The context makes it very clear that He is not referring to His second coming, but rather to the presence and ministry of the Holy Spirit among His people in the Church age. The Church is not an orphanage (a home for children without parents); but to the degree we do not receive and submit to the Holy Spirit's ministry in our midst, we are an orphanage! Why? Because His ministry is to reveal our Father to us! In some places, for all intents and purposes, the Church seems orphaned, with the "ministers" of the Church acting as its "caretakers." Thus many fail to enjoy the present aspect of their inheritance.

But the Scriptures promise us something far superior to an orphanage, it is the family of God! The primary difference between a family and an orphanage is the active presence of a parent or parents with the children. What have we substituted for His operative parental presence in our midst? For example, a degree in theology is no substitute for the anointing to minister the word of God. A degree in theology is not necessarily bad, but it can never replace God's anointing. One can be highly educated, and yet not be anointed to teach the Scriptures. The reverse can also be true. One can be uneducated and yet be mightily anointed by God. My point is that God's approval of one's ministry is not based on human criteria. To the degree we substitute a standard other than God's, we have an orphanage! If in evaluating or instituting leadership (or anything else in the Church), we use man's standards rather than God's, we tell God we do not need His perspective on the matter.

This is precisely what the Pharisees confronted Jesus with during His earthly ministry. Their basic attitude was, "We don't need you; You don't fit into our program." Their religious system with all their "holy" activities was an orphanage! The glory of the Father was not in their midst. When He reached down to them as the Son, they found Him too upsetting to their "normal" way of functioning. The cost was too high for them to make the transition into family. Too much would have to change for *God* to be at home in their midst. For us, the issue is not how at home *we* are in our local church, but how at home He is. How well does *He* fit in? The Pharisees settled for a religious system instead of the family of God.

"O Jerusalem, Jerusalem, who kills the prophets and stones those who are sent to her! How often I wanted to gather your children together, the way a hen gathers her chicks under her wings, and you were unwilling. Behold your house is being left to you desolate!" (Matt. 23:37,38)

Notice, the temple was *being* left desolate as Jesus departed. The glory and presence of God was leaving, and most people did not understand what was happening.

Today, He is again coming to His people in the power of His Holy Spirit for the purpose of establishing the family of God. In His family, He is to be central, with His presence filling His house. When we His children come together, it is for us to grow in our love for Him and each other. If He is not given His rightful place in our midst, He will deal with us as He endeavors to draw us into greater intimacy with Him. But if we do not respond, then we will find ourselves increasingly more comfortable in *our* ways of doing things, and finally, we will not even notice when He slips out the door. I am not referring to Christians losing their salvation, but losing the privilege of finding their unique place in God's family. Today, in many places He is bringing His children together around His presence. Creeds are not the focus; neither are forms of worship, modes of dress, denominational affiliation, etc. As people respond to His wooing, they see an interesting phenomenon; *it is the family of God!*

The Spirit we have received is the One Who places sons (HUIOTHESIA). There is an inner tugging that each of us has experienced ever since we were filled with the Holy Spirit. It is a drawing toward intimacy with God and with His people. That inner tugging is, in fact, the longing of God within us for the reality of His family to be established in the earth! One can be a Christian and yet not be walking in the *practical* reality of this family.

"For all who are being led by the Spirit of God, these are sons [HUIOS] of God." (Rom. 8:14)

Notice the consequence of the Spirit's leading these sons of God.

"For you have not received a spirit of slavery leading to fear again, but you have received a spirit of adoption as sons [HUIOTHESIA] by which we cry out, 'Abba! Father!'" (Rom. 8:15)

The Spirit of God is leading His people into a unique placement that each one has in His family *whereby we cry out in recognition and enjoyment of His fatherhood.* That is why Paul's statement is so significant.

"In love He predestined us to adoption as sons [HUIO-THESIA] through Jesus Christ to *Himself,* according to the kind intention of His will." (Eph. 1:5, emphasis mine)

The truth concerning God's family contains within it His call to His people to come *unto Him!* As we gather in His presence, we will find others there also crying, "My Dad, my Father." What a joy! We have been predestined to participate in the glorious reality of God's family on the earth. And this is but a taste of the fullness we will know in the full manifestation of His glory at the end of the age.

# Chapter 7

# He Predestined Us to Adoption as Sons II

"In love He˘ predestined us to adoption as sons through Jesus Christ to Himself, according to the kind intention of His will." (Eph. 1:5)

"Sonship" is not a term that conveys independence; rather it points us to the subject of family. It is not a word that one can use to justify being a spiritual "hermit," i.e., one who sits off by himself endeavoring to be spiritually mature without the rest of the Body of Christ. One who thinks he does not need the rest of the Church because he has achieved "sonship," is not responding to the Spirit of God. The Spirit we have received seeks to place us as sons (HUIOTHESIA) in very practical ways in His family. What are the implications of being strategically placed in God's family? Foremost in importance is the truth of *the fatherhood of God.* God is our Father.

The most common term Jesus used when referring to God was "Father." God was His Father, and He is ours as well. He told us to pray recognizing our sonship.

"Our Father who art in heaven..." (Matt.6:9)

As we consider the relationship Jesus had with His Father, we receive insight into the kind of relationship we are to have with Him as well. *Jesus is the perfect example of sonship!* Jesus loved His Father and walked in intimacy with Him. God, in turn, was blessed with and pleased in His Son. From the beginning, Jesus was consumed with the things of His Father. We see this even in His youth, as He amazed the teachers in the temple with His understanding at the age of twelve. When Mary and Joseph found Him they were astonished, too.

"...and His mother said to Him, 'Son, why have you treated us this way? Behold, Your father and I have been anxiously looking for You.' " (Luke 2:48)

Mary seemed confused. After all she had been through, surely she knew better than to refer to Joseph as Jesus' father. Her experiences were many: the Holy Spirit Who caused her to conceive as a virgin, the visit of the angel Gabriel, the shepherds who saw a vision of the angelic hosts, the wise men, the star over the place of Jesus' birth, Simeon's declaration that now he had seen the salvation of God, etc. Perhaps time had dimmed the impact of her experiences. We do not know, but Jesus' immediate response was to point to His *heavenly* Father.

"He said to them, 'Why is it that you were looking for Me? Did you not know that I had to be in My Father's house [lit. in the things of My Father.]?' " (Luke 2:49)

Maybe this was the first time He had spoken this way. It seems as though something had changed in His relationship with Mary and Joseph. Apparently He was now speaking of His relationship with His heavenly Father more openly than before.

"And they did not understand the statement which He had made to them. And He went down with them, and came to Nazareth; and He continued in subjection to them; and His mother treasured all these things in her heart. And Jesus kept increasing in wisdom and stature, and in favor with God and men." (Luke 2:50-52)

The fact that Jesus increased in favor with God, does not indicate an increase of God's love for His Son. The Father had loved His Son eternally! Rather it reveals a relationship that was dynamic and maturing! Jesus *grew* in the scope of His obedience as He walked with God.

"He humbled Himself *by becoming obedient* to the point of death, even death on a cross." (Phil. 2:8, emphasis mine)

"Although He was a Son, He *learned obedience* from the things which He suffered." (Heb. 5:8, emphasis mine)

This is not to imply that Jesus was ever disobedient. He was always perfectly obedient; He always did the will of His Father. But as Jesus grew, the Father required more of His

Son. Jesus' heart was "stretched" to embrace these greater requirements. As He perfectly obeyed His Father in each case, His capacity to express His Father grew as well. This was a process of growth for Jesus; *it is a pattern for our growth!* Then one day came the supreme test; the Father pointed His Son to Calvary! There Jesus' heart was stretched so far it broke. But He perfectly obeyed His Father even then. The cross is the example of obedience in its highest form! This is why we are to be...

"...conformed to His death." (Phil. 3:10)

Jesus' earthly relationship with His Father was not static. As He grew in the favor of God, He was actually maturing for His ministry. Jesus, the child, was being prepared for His adult role as Messiah. Then on the day of His baptism...

"...a voice came out of heaven, 'Thou art My beloved Son, in Thee I am well pleased.' " (Luke 3:22)

At this point the Father declared His Son's readiness for the next phase of ministry. All that Jesus had walked in up to this point was crucial in His training. He had not come to earth just to do a simple task. He had come to reveal Someone, and to do so accurately. Thus He learned to spend time in His Father's presence as a child. *He was the perfect Son before He did any public ministry,* and because He was the perfect Son, He was able to say,

"He who has seen Me has seen the Father; how do you say, 'Show us the Father'? Do you not believe that I am in the Father, and the Father is in Me? The words that I say to you I do not speak on My own initiative, but the Father abiding in Me does His works. Believe Me that I am in the Father, and the Father in Me." (Jn. 14:9-11)

It is absolutely crucial that we see the Father as we view the Son. His ministry to men depended upon His being an accurate representation of the One who had sent Him. He would have been totally unsuccessful in His ministry if He had misrepresented His Father in even the smallest way. Some cults teach that Jesus is less than God, but the Deity of Christ is crucial to sound theology. If we dishonor the Son, we dishonor the One who sent Him (Jn. 5:23)!

Jesus was the Son of God before He was revealed as Messiah. "Sonship" refers to His relationship to His Father; "Messiahship" refers to His ministry to men. *"Son" refers to who He was; "Messiah" refers to what He did, based on who He was.* Therefore His ministry to men rested on the foundation of His relationship to His Father. This is where satan began his attack. He did not say, "If You are the Messiah of Israel, turn these stones into bread." Rather he said, "If You are the Son of God, turn these stones into bread." If satan had undermined that truth, he would have won the whole war! Jesus clearly understood His sonship and, secure in His identity, He conquered the powers of darkness in His ministry as the Messiah.

Herein lies a principle of victory for us. Overcoming the enemy rests on the foundation of seeing our sonship. The key is not primarily that we see our ministry. Our focus must be our relationship with God upon which our ministry rests! *Ministry is the consequence of walking in sonship.* "Sonship" has to do not only with our relationship with God, but with our spiritual brothers and sisters as well. *The family of God is God's end-time weapon for the final crushing of satan!*

"And the God of peace will soon crush Satan under your feet." (Rom. 16:20)

"For all who are being led by the Spirit of God, these are sons of God." (Rom. 8:14)

Christians reveal their maturity in so far as they are led by the Spirit of God. When He has *His* way in us, that is sonship in action! Ministry then, is the consequence of people knowing who they are and following the Spirit's leading. This serves to crush the power of the enemy both in their own lives, as well as in the lives of others.

Many of God's people wonder whether they are called to be pastors, evangelists, teachers, prophets or apostles. But these giftings are few in the Church compared with the over-all number of God's people. Whereas most will not be a pastor or a teacher, sonship is held out for all! The fruit-fulness of our ministry depends on how well we walk as sons with our heavenly Father, and as brothers or sisters with our brethren. The Family of God is key to the fulfillment of God's purposes in these days. This is why Paul says,

"In love He predestined us to adoption as sons [HUIO-THESIA] through Jesus Christ to Himself, according to the kind intention of His will." (Eph. 1:5)

Today God is strategically placing each son in His family where each one can lay hold of the inheritance and ministry that is theirs in this generation.

# Chapter 8

# According to the Kind Intention of His Will

"He predestined us to adoption as sons through Jesus Christ to Himself, according to the kind intention [lit. good pleasure] of His will." (Eph. 1:5)

God intends good things for us and it is His *pleasure* to bring them to pass. It does not bring Him pain to be involved with His people. In fact, He is excited as He prepares the Bride of Christ for her marriage supper with the Lamb. God does not need to "have His arm twisted" to move on our behalf. It was His good pleasure to choose us in the first place! Before we knew Him, before we were aware of His existence, while we were living for ourselves in all manner of sin, God was pleased to call us to Himself and destine us to enjoy full standing in His family! This means we are called to be sons in line for an inheritance that has been promised not only to us, but also to the First-born, the Lord Jesus Christ. We are joint heirs with Him.

As we consider the Father's great love and commitment to His Son Jesus, we receive insight into His heart of love for us.

"He who has My commandments and keeps them, he it is who loves Me; and he who loves Me shall be loved by My Father, and I will love him, and will disclose Myself to him." (Jn. 14:21)

Jesus said He would reveal Himself to those who loved Him. In other words, lovers of Jesus would recognize His Lordship and His role as Messiah of Israel. Only *they* would have clear insight into His person. This exclusive disclosure, however, brought great concern to one of His listeners.

"Judas (not Iscariot) said to Him, 'Lord, what then has happened that You are going to disclose Yourself to us, and not to the world?' " (Jn. 14:22)

The general thought of the day was that when the Messiah was revealed, it would be to the whole world! Everyone would recognize Him and honor Him as King of the nations. Many Old Testament scriptures seemed to confirm this line of thought. However, Jesus did not respond to Judas' theology; He simply reiterated what He had just said.

"...'If anyone loves Me, he will keep My word; and My Father will love him, and We will come to him, and make our abode with him.' " (Jn. 14:23)

The promise here is that there would come an abiding presence of God in the lives of those loving the Lord Jesus.

God *committed Himself* to abide with those who are in love with His Son. And God takes His commitments seriously!

"If God is for us, who is against us?" (Rom. 8:31)

God does not need to be motivated in order to be committed to us; but *we* need to be exhorted to rise up and follow *Him* in what *He* is doing in the earth! We can see this throughout history. Repeatedly God sent men to stir His people to action. Usually they needed to repent of idolatry or other sinful activity. The problem was never that God needed to turn toward man. It was always His people that needed to turn toward Him!

Concerning our Lord's heart for the house of God, the Scriptures say,

"Zeal for Thy house will consume Me." (Jn. 2:17)

This statement describes more than just Jesus' feelings at the time of His earthly ministry. It also gives us God's *eternal* perspective. Though it is true that Jesus' zeal for the house of God brought Him into conflict with the religious leaders of His day, it is also true that His zeal caused Him to come to earth in the first place! As He ministered among the Jewish people, His zeal for the house of God consumed Him. This was but a reflection of what He had felt from all eternity! Hundreds of years earlier, Isaiah had prophesied that a child would be born who would be called the Wonderful Counselor, Mighty God, Everlasting Father, etc. The government would rest upon His shoulders and of its increase there would be no end. Then Isaiah boldly declares,

"The zeal of the Lord of hosts will accomplish this." (Isa. 9:7)

Now that the price has been paid to establish the foundation of His house, has God's zeal diminished? The answer must be a resounding, "no," until the whole purpose of God is accomplished!

One might ask, "Is not intercession a picture of people endeavoring to move God to action?" Not really. In fact, those who are burdened to intercede and cry out to God concerning needs they see, are testimonies of His zeal! The burden they carry is the burden of *the Lord!* Anointed intercession is not people trying to get God to do something; it is God moving upon people and allowing them to participate in His burden. As they cry out, the voice of our High Priest, who ever lives to make intercession for us, can be heard in their prayers! The Good Shepherd can be seen in part through pastoral ministry in the Church, just as Christ the Teacher can be seen in part through teaching ministry in the Church. In the same way our great High Priest is expressed in part as Christians move in the spirit of intercession! God is pleased to be involved with His people.

"He predestined us to adoption as sons through Jesus
Christ to Himself, according to the kind intention [good
pleasure] of His will." (Eph. 1:5)

From this verse we recognize that God *was* pleased to choose us and destine us beforehand (predestine us) to become placed (adopted) as sons in His family. Nothing has changed. He *continues* to be pleased and zealously involved in an on-going way in our lives, as He brings us to the fulfillment of His plan.

This involvement of a holy God with such a people as we are is certainly...

"...to the praise of the glory of His grace, which He freely bestowed on us in the Beloved." (Eph. 1:6)

The fact that, despite all our stumblings and failures (past and present ones!) God could still *take pleasure* in us, indicates a *glory* to His grace that demands our attention! Those who see the magnitude of their sin will grasp the magnitude of God's grace in loving them. When one considers his personal sin to be small and insignificant, he will also see God's grace in the same way. But when one is awestruck by the horror of his sin and the holiness of God, he can agree with Isaiah,

> "Woe is me, for I am ruined! Because I am a man of unclean lips, and I live among a people of unclean lips; for my eyes have seen the King, the Lord of hosts." (Isa. 6:5)

Against a backdrop of such contrast (the extreme wickedness of sin and the extreme holiness of God), grace shines with a glory that stuns the rational mind! Our praise is to be offered to Him according to the *glory* of His grace!

God's grace is not small and insignificant. When we consider the expanse of the gap that separated us from God, the greatness of our sin, and the purity of His holiness, we are overwhelmed! We had no means for reconciliation with Him from our side of the chasm. There was only hopelessness and despair. Then we saw His hand reaching toward us, not clenched in anger, but open, seeking to hold us. When we realized it was bloody and wounded, it dawned on us that grace is far greater then we ever imagined. It is not God's offer to just help us a little in our problems; *grace is expressed in the fact that He crossed the gap and allowed our wickedness to be placed on Him!* The effect that had on Him cannot be grasped by our finite minds! But because He did take our sins upon Himself, we no longer find guilt and condemnation when we stand before Him. Having touched infinite love, we can never be the same. *Thankfulness will characterize those who see these things.* Thus, our praise and worship, reflecting the magnitude of what has occurred, *spring forth in a way befitting the glory* of His grace.

Many Christians it seems, do not worship God with understanding. If our worship is absent-minded or long-faced, lacking joy, perhaps we need to examine again the magnitude of what God has done! Only eternity will enable us to express *fully* our gratitude for this great salvation. Until then, let us *grow* in our thanksgiving, responding to the glory of His grace!

> "In love He predestined us to adoption as sons through Jesus Christ to Himself, according to the kind intention of His will, to the praise of the glory of His grace, which He freely bestowed on us in the Beloved." (Eph. 1:5,6)

**Chapter 9**

# We Have Redemption
# Through His Blood

"In Him we have redemption through His blood, the
forgiveness of our trespasses, according to the riches of
His grace." (Eph. 1:7)

One of the scourges of our civilization today is terrorism.
Planes are hijacked, busloads of children are commandeered,
innocent people are kidnaped and held captive for a price.
Not until the ransom is paid (be it money, publicity for a
cause, the freeing of other terrorists from prison or some
other demand) are the victims released.

Mankind is also subject to another kind of terrorism. It is
referred to in the word "redemption," which in the Greek
means "release effected by payment of a ransom." We were
captives, unable to free ourselves from sin, which held us in
bondage. Now we have been released through the payment
of a particular price—the blood of Jesus!

On the other hand, all who are not redeemed continue to

be held captive by the power of sin, and the Law plays a key role in that captivity.

"The sting of death is sin, and *the power of sin is the Law.*" (1 Cor. 15:56, emphasis mine)

Sin rules in human lives through God's Law. Obviously, sin did not come from the Law; it originated with man through Adam's fall. However, while the Law did originate in God, it was not given as a solution to the sin problem. It was to point out sin in our lives. The Law and sin combined to be a burden greater than man could bear, resulting in despair and hopelessness (Rom. 7:24).

"Or do you not know, brethren (for I am speaking to those who know the Law), that the Law has jurisdiction over a person as long as he lives? For the married woman is bound by law to her husband while he is living; but if her husband dies, she is released from the law concerning the husband. So then if, while her husband is living, she is joined to another man, she shall be called an adulteress; but if her husband dies, she is free from the law, so that she is not an adulteress, though she is joined to another man. Therefore, my brethren, you also were made to die to the Law through the body of Christ, that you might be joined to another, to Him who was raised from the dead, that we might bear fruit for God." (Rom. 7:1-4)

Using marriage as an analogy, Paul establishes a significant truth concerning our relationship with the Law. We were joined to the Law. The only way for us to be freed was to die to it and be joined to another, to Him who was raised from the dead, the Lord Jesus! Christianity is not to be a relationship of people with laws, rules and regulations; rather it is a people joined with a person! We are in union with someone.

"But the one who joins himself to the Lord is one spirit with Him." (1 Cor. 6:17)

The purpose of this union is that we might bear fruit for God. Religion is the product of union with law; spiritual fruit is the product of union with the Lord Jesus. Jesus referred to this relationship when He said that if we abide in Him (in His presence and His word), we would bear much fruit and so prove to be His disciples. This is God's desire for our lives. However, instead of fruit, He often finds religious practices and an emphasis on external conformity to truth. Many Christians walk in an Old Testament type of mentality with God. Their lives portray human attempts at holiness. In their thinking, the Bible is "a list of do's and don'ts." They are joined in mental relationship with a book (the Bible), instead of in a heart relationship with the One who wrote it!

One can know a great deal about apples; but that in itself does not produce apples. Fruit is the product of life, not of knowledge. It takes a unique life, dormant within an apple seed to produce a tree that will ultimately bear *bushels* of apples! When people are rooted in a *living* relationship with Christ, there *will be* results (Bible reading, witnessing, serving one another, godly character, etc.). Without life union and relationship with Him, we bear counterfeit "apples"! A plastic apple may look terrific; however, I would not try to eat one! Nor would I attempt to grow new apple trees from one! Why? There is no reproductive life in it. Men can manufacture plastic apples; only Jesus' life can produce spiritual fruit that brings God the glory He deserves.

"For while we were in the flesh, the sinful passions, which were aroused by the Law, were at work in the members of our body to bear fruit for death." (Rom. 7:5)

When one is in bondage to sin, he cannot bring forth the fruit of righteousness, and the Law is no solution to his problem. Instead of fruitfulness, death is established in us. What is seen in our lives testifies to the death within. The Law only serves to *arouse* our sinful passions.

"But now we have been released from the Law, having died to that by which we were bound, so that we serve in newness of the Spirit and not in oldness of the letter." (Rom. 7:6)

Once we have been released from the Law, our service to God is no longer to be based on the letter of God's word, but in newness of the Spirit. It is to have the freshness of God's anointing oil on it! Christian lives are not to be stale. The spontaneous joy of hearing and responding to Him is to permeate our service. Parents understand the difference in attitude when their children desire to do a particular task and when they do not. "Foot dragging" is one sign of a reluctant response. There are many "foot draggers" in Christendom. "Well, all right if its really necessary, I'll be there." "Do I have to do that (tithe, attend meetings, witness, serve others, etc.) in order to go to heaven"? Such words reflect serving in the oldness of the letter. God is not satisfied when we do only what we know we should; He wants to elevate us into a *New Testament kind of serving!* This kind of serving is not limited to what is required in a written commandment; rather, it is in the newness of a Spirit-filled relationship that *fulfills* what is written! Our lives are to harmonize with the Scriptures. However, this will not be accomplished by a grudging, "what is required of me" attitude. It will be established by our being continually filled with the same Spirit who *wrote* the requirements in the first place!

Jesus set us free through redemption in order for us to serve Him in a way that expresses His kingdom, i.e., righteousness, peace and joy *in the Holy Spirit.* To be justified through Jesus' blood and then use human efforts to do God's will actually negates the message. When Christians serve in their own strength, it will not be long before their joy and peace in doing His will diminishes. Thus there is not an expression of God's kingdom. Many new Christians start out with great zeal for God, but "burn out" within a few years. What has been exhibited is the "staying power" of their personalities in light of their initial experience with Christ. Some have greater "staying power" than others. However, God's kingdom cannot be built on the strength of His people's personalities. There will always be times of discouragement; but there is also a Fountain that never runs dry! As we continually come and drink of His life, learning to abide in His presence, *the staying power of His life becomes the foundation upon which His purposes are established in our lives.* The joy of serving Him comes from spending time with Him whom we serve! If we do not make His presence a priority for our time, the *task* will become our major focus rather than the One who commissioned us. Ministry alone can bring a fleeting joy; Jesus is joy itself. The power of God's kingdom is not His law, but *His presence!* Let us give ourselves wholeheartedly to Him, thankful for His great gift of redemption. Then *He* will gain the glory as *we* live righteous and godly lives in union with Him by the strength that *He* supplies. In so doing, we will live by the power of the ages to come and bring it to bear on this present age.

# Chapter 10

# According to the Riches of His Grace

"In Him we have redemption through His blood, the forgiveness of our trespasses, according to the riches of His grace, which He lavished upon us." (Eph. 1:7,8)

Our redemption, the forgiveness of our sins, is granted according to the *riches* of God's grace which He *lavished* upon us. This verse indicates God's overwhelming supply for meeting the need of man. Where the Church fails to understand the grace of God, we always find spiritual poverty. The wealth of God is found in His grace. When we compare the life and ministry of the Lord Jesus in the gospels, or the early Church in the book of Acts, with the Church today, it is clear there are riches in God *we are not laying hold of.* There are dimensions of insight, wisdom, revelation and power that God wants to release among us. One reason He cannot do so is because we fail to see the riches of His grace available to us in Christ. We will not apprehend our inheritance by striving after it in our own strength! We must *receive* by faith what God has already declared to be ours! The life of a godly man will reflect the grace of God, not his own religious abilities. Everything from the forgiveness of sins (our standing in Christ) to ministry (our walking with Christ) is the product of grace. God wants us to appropriate His grace for enablement to express His life to our generation. *Only His grace is sufficient for the task!*

> "As to this salvation, the prophets who prophesied of the grace that would come to you made careful search and inquiry, seeking to know what person or time the Spirit of Christ within them was indicating as He predicted the sufferings of Christ and the glories to follow." (1 Pet. 1:10,11)

Prophets in the Old Testament spoke of a day when the grace of God would come to a people on the earth. These prophets sought insight as the Spirit of God testified through them that the Messiah would come and endure great suffering, after which there would be a time of great glory. The glories to follow are clearly seen in the Book of Acts. From the beginning of the Church, God's power was evident among His people. Thousands were saved in a single day. Miracles and healings occurred as the religious system was shaken by divine visitation. What a glorious beginning!

Unfortunately, as we examine Church history, we find progressive decline in spiritual quality in concert with a growth in organized institutionalism. Even as early as the first century, spiritual decay had set in. Chapters two and three of Revelation were specifically directed toward churches that had drifted from the roots of their beginnings. The church at Ephesus had fallen from her first love. Those at Pergamum had problems because of an infiltration of the teachings of Balaam and the Nicolaitans. Thyatira was involved with a false prophetess named Jezebel. Nor did the record improve with age.

In fact as Christianity grew in the earth, as God's people increased in acceptability and popularity in the eyes of the world, something was lost of heaven's life and anointing. Over the years, the Church became more an institution filled with external form than a family filled with the presence of God. Where did we miss it? Somewhere along the line, *we failed to understand the grace of God. All the wealth of heaven is only available through His grace!*

The most significant reason Christians fail to appropriate grace is failure to see their tremendous need for it! The Kingdom of God can only be extended in the earth through God's ability. If we believe something can be accomplished through our strength, we will generate multitudes of ideas and programs to help God fulfill His purpose. We will train leaders *how to do things,* rather than how to abide in Christ and rely on His strength! This has been a basic problem in the Church throughout history. Men make decisions and then ask God to bless their plans, instead of seeking His mind and then implementing in obedience what He reveals. The Kingdom of God is expressed through *His* initiative and our obedience. This is how His rule is extended in and through us. When men initiate some action, the result may look good externally, and God may even bless and use some of what is done. However, the end product will be a mixture. It may appear very successful in the eyes of men, and yet be a failure in God's sight and, in the long run, have an ineffective impact upon the world. To many, the Church today is seen as a great and powerful institution that is basically irrelevant to the major problems facing mankind. What a contrast to the first century. The Church was a people filled with the Holy Spirit, who turned the then-known world "upside down" with the message about the King.

What is the desire of our hearts? Respectability in the eyes of men, or the extension of God's kingdom? What do we want? Success as defined by man's standard, or the favor that comes from God's approval? What God approves of will have issued forth from His life and grace. What men endorse is what seems appropriate and is comfortable to them. We desperately need to learn God's ways in order that we grow increasingly comfortable in what He is doing, and uncomfortable in what originates from man. Only the riches of His grace and power will bring this generation into the Kingdom of God.

As the prophets sought to understand God's purpose, He revealed that His grace would be poured out on His people. The Spirit within them predicted that their Messiah would suffer for them and that great glories would follow. In light of these things, Peter tells us to do three things.

First, gird your minds for action. Often when the message of grace is preached and we are told that apart from Him we can do nothing, our tendency is to sit back and *expect to do nothing!* Of course, if that is our expectation then, according to our faith, that is exactly what will happen! If we settle back, enjoying God's forgiveness, we will fail to affect the world around us! Obviously, this is not how the early Church lived. Girding our minds for action means that as God's truth is revealed to us, we should expect Him to "open doors" for us and set up situations where we will be able to put into practice what He has just revealed! We are not to simply file His instructions away in notebooks (girding our minds for filing). Rather we are to let God use us in practical and concrete ways to minister the truth He has been teaching us. Girding our minds for action does not mean we are to initiate some activity in God's name; rather, it indicates *a holy expectation and faith in God the initiator!* He will give us opportunities to apply what He has said. Expect action! Look for His initiative! Watch for the open doors!

Secondly, be sober in spirit. The word "sober" means, free from the influence of intoxicants. When one is under the influence of an intoxicant such as alcohol, his faculties are impaired. He is unable to interact appropriately with his surroundings. There is a dullness of mind, a lack of clarity in thought, and he relates to those around him with a "who cares" attitude. However, Peter says we are to keep sober in spirit. In other words, if our minds are expecting action, then our spirits must be "fine tuned" and sensitive to the Spirit of God as He shows us what to do. I wonder how many opportunities to minister the life of the Lord Jesus we have missed because we were distracted by the things of this life? Often, we are so caught up with what we see that we are too dull in our spirits to sense the eternal realities of God's life and purpose as well as satan's opposition. In order to walk sober in spirit, we must be "fine tuned" or "sharpened" in our inner man. Our prayer ought to be that God would increase our sensitivity to His voice.

Thirdly, you must fix your hope completely on the grace to be brought to you at the revelation of Jesus. What a powerful statement! The grace of God brought Jesus to the earth the first time. When He came, He was filled with grace and truth (Jn. 1:14). When He ascended, He poured (lavished) the riches of His grace upon us. Grace upon grace upon grace! That is our hope in this age! This verse indicates there is even more! At the greatest revelation of Jesus in history (His second coming), there will be *the greatest outpouring of His grace in history!* Just think! There will be instant resurrection and glorification for millions of people simultaneously! The grace to be manifested then, will be the same grace God has lavished upon us today. However, there will be more of it! Therefore, to have our hope fixed completely on the grace to be brought to us, means we are to fix our hope on the grace He *has already lavished* upon us. We live and move and have our being both now and in eternity to come by the grace of God. We must learn to live in and draw from the wealth of that grace!

"In Him we have redemption through His blood, the forgiveness of our trespasses, according to the riches of His grace, which He lavished upon us." (Eph. 1:7,8)

# Chapter 11

# Making Known to Us the Mystery of His Will

"In all wisdom and insight He made known [lit. *making known*] to us the mystery of His will, according to His kind intention which He purposed in Him." (Eph. 1:8,9, emphasis mine)

God's will is a mystery that is *progressively* being made known to His people. We do not know every detail of His plan concerning our future; we know in part. However, He desires to reveal His truth to us as we humble ourselves before Him. Truth is hidden that it might be revealed to those who seek Him. The Lord Jesus demonstrated this when He spoke in parables so the proud could not understand what He was saying. That was His "kingdom strategy," i.e., His strategy for establishing the Kingdom of God on earth. His approach has not changed!

"And the disciples came and said to Him, 'Why do You speak to them in parables?' And He answered and said to them, 'To you it has been granted to know the mysteries of the kingdom of heaven, but to them it has not been granted. And in their case the prophecy of Isaiah is being fulfilled, which says, "You will keep on hearing, but will not understand; and you will keep on seeing, but will not perceive; for the heart of this people has become dull, and with their ears they scarcely hear, and they have closed their eyes lest they should see with their eyes, and hear with their ears, and understand with their heart and return, and I should heal them." But blessed are your eyes, because they see; and your ears, because they hear.' " (Matt. 13:10,11,14-16)

It is a sign of judgment when people cannot hear God's truth; and it is a sign of God's grace when they do. The twelve apostles were able to hear because it had been *granted* to them! God the Father had specifically shown to Jesus those men who were to be named as apostles (Luke 6:12,13), and thus the Son knew that God had granted them grace to hear. On the other hand, when speaking to the multitudes, He would say,

"He *who has ears,* let him hear." (Matt. 13:9, emphasis mine)

Among the multitudes, there were those who had "ears to hear," but there were many others who did not. Those whose hearts were sensitive to the Spirit of God grasped the message of the kingdom; for others, the truth passed right by them! They heard ( physically), but they did not understand. This was God's kingdom strategy, and it remains so today! The meek will hear, understand and ultimately inherit the earth. The arrogant will not!

How is one able to tell if another has really heard (in his heart) the message of the kingdom or not? If his life continues on the same as before, he has not heard! If one sees changes, and I am referring to heart changes, not necessarily external ones, then hearing is taking place. Sometimes people clearly hear the convicting message of God's kingdom in their hearts, but do not immediately change. Yet deep inside, they have been pierced to the heart. The Spirit of God has deeply convicted them. They walk away unable to shake the feeling that He is real and is pursuing them! Change has begun! It will not be external at first, but something is happening. That person must now deal with what he has heard deep inside, *knowing that it is truth!* At this point, the man is changing within and his unsaved friends cannot figure out what is happening to him. It is a mystery. It is the Kingdom of God being established in their friend. They cannot know because...

"...unless one is born again, he cannot see the Kingdom of God." (Jn. 3:3)

Multitudes of people today are totally unaware of God's kingdom in its present expression. However, it is as real (even more so) than the visible material nations making up this earth. God, His kingdom, His will and His purposes are *hidden that they might be revealed.* Those who are proud and arrogant will not understand the Kingdom of God even as it is extended right in their midst! Jesus said,

"I praise Thee, O Father, Lord of heaven and earth, that Thou didst hide these things from the wise and intelligent and didst reveal them to babes." (Matt. 11:25)

Those with the greatest knowledge of the Scriptures (the Pharisees and Sadducees) had the most difficulty with the truths of the Kingdom. Scripture says,

"Knowledge makes arrogant, but love [Greek AGAPE] edifies." (1 Cor. 8:1)

Love (Greek AGAPE) is the most succinct description of God (1 Jn. 4:8). Love defines His character. Knowledge *about* God can be intellectually stimulating, but God desires His character to be worked into our lives. Our tendency, however, has been to substitute knowledge *about* God for knowledge *of* God. It is a poor substitute. Knowing Him intimately is the essence of Christianity. Jesus said,

"You are My friends, if you do what I command you." (Jn. 15:14)

In effect, what He said was, "You can have with Me what Abraham had in the Old Testament." Abraham walked in a friendship relationship with the Lord. The same was true of Moses (Ex. 33:11). A common significant characteristic of these two men was that God included them in the secrets of His heart. They were welcomed into the councils of the Almighty! He unveiled to them many things that other men did not know or understand. He let them see something of His plan and purpose. He let them experience a little of what He felt on certain issues. When the time was ripe for judgment upon Sodom and Gomorrah, God did not destroy them without first consulting His friend Abraham (Gen. 18).

Consider Moses. One of the distinguishing marks of his life was the precision with which he built the house of God in his generation. This accuracy did not come from books, a college education, or methods he learned from other men. It came from being in the presence of God on the mountain! This is not to say that books are not helpful, or that education is wrong. But *such things can never take the place of being in the presence of God, as Moses was on the mountain!*

The Jewish people found their national identity by looking to Abraham and Moses. They saw themselves as "the seed of Abraham" and custodians of the Law as revealed to Moses. Yet they missed a key issue. Abraham and Moses were *friends of God!* The Jewish people accepted what Abraham and Moses said, but by and large they did not seek the relationship with God that these two great patriarchs had.

It can be easy to walk in the "glow" of a man who has stood in the presence of God, and not take time to pursue the One who anointed him! It is healthy for God's people to identify with certain Christian leaders and their ministries. God blesses and edifies His people through godly leadership in the Church. However, it is possible to enjoy the things of God without taking time to enjoy the God of the things! Too many Christians are learning *about God, instead of becoming friends of God!* As a result, His will for their *personal* lives remains a mystery. They may understand His general will (read the Bible, be faithful to their spouse, be committed to a local church, etc.). Concerning direction for their personal lives and ministries, however, God's will is something of a mystery. Insight comes from friendship with God!

"You are My friends, if you do what I command you."
(Jn. 15:14)

If we respond to what He is saying, He will bring us into
friendship with Him.

"No longer do I call you slaves, for the slave does not
know what his master is doing; but I have called you
friends, for all things that I have heard from My Father
I have made known to you." (Jn. 15:15)

God includes His friends in the secrets of His heart. He
welcomes them into the councils of the Almighty and gives
them insights into the mysteries of His kingdom.

Today there is a mixture of voices going forth in the
Name of Jesus. Many Christians run after messages that
have questionable value in the Spirit. Deception is not
decreasing; it is increasing. The way to spot a counterfeit is
to spend time with the Author of the genuine. He promises
to reveal His will to us in such a way that we will understand it and be able to embrace it. He knows our personalities, our tendencies and our weaknesses. He knows how to
deal intimately in our lives. *He knows how to best reveal
truth to us so we can recognize it is from Him.* That is why
Paul says,

"*In all wisdom and insight* He made known [lit. making
known] to us the mystery of His will, according to His
kind intention which He purposed in Him." (Eph. 1:8,9,
emphasis mine)

Our hope does not lie in our ability to hear Him; *it is in*

*Him and His wisdom and ability to reveal His truth to us.*
What is the key to a sound Christian life-style? It is in being
a friend of God.

# Chapter 12

# According to His Kind Intention

"In all wisdom and insight He made known to us the mystery of His will, according to His kind intention [lit. good pleasure] which He purposed in Him." (Eph. 1:8,9)

Long ago God purposed to accomplish something in Christ and today we see it being worked out in our time-space world. His design involved the incarnation, death and resurrection of His Son. The whole of Church history is also a testimony to this glorious plan (Pentecost, His dealings with man throughout the ages, including today as He prepares His bride for the appearing of her majestic Bridegroom). All events lead toward a working out of His purpose, that which reflects His good pleasure. In other words, it expresses the desire of His heart, something He has longed for from eternity. Today, many who are familiar with Church history fail to see His strategy that was behind the facts. What did He intend? What was the root of His activities in the earth?

To begin to unravel the mystery of His will, we must be aware of the first objective of our call in God. It is not a call to reach unbelievers, or to have some ministry in the Church. Our primary call is to *Him!*

"God is faithful, through whom you were *called into fellowship with His Son, Jesus Christ our Lord.*" (1 Cor. 1:9, emphasis mine)

"And you shall receive the gift of the Holy Spirit. For the promise is for you and your children, and for all who are far off, as many as the Lord our God shall call to *Himself.*" (Acts 2:38,39, emphasis mine)

If we have not responded to this, we will misinterpret His activities in the earth. We may participate in what He is doing without understanding His purpose in our generation! His plan is hidden within *the pleasure of His heart!* If we do not have an intimate relationship with Him, how can we know what pleases Him? Some will say His greatest joy is to see His house built correctly. Others say it is to win the lost. Still others would point to worship. All of these are correct, yet each is incomplete. Even when considered together, these answers are not sufficient. There is one thing that uniquely delights God's heart. *It is His Son! The Lord Jesus!*

Let us briefly look at these particular answers:

**Correct building.** One can develop a seemingly biblical building methodology concerning the Church without drawing his life from union with the Lord Jesus ( being more "book-centered" than "Christ centered").

**Witnessing.** One can be very active in witnessing to the unsaved with his activities predominantly being "dead works" (his outreach is not generated by union with the Lord Jesus). Some share with others because they do not feel secure in God's love and seek to earn it through their efforts. It is quite different when one shares the gospel being secure in God's favor and sensing His anointing.

**Worship.** Worship can be resounding and harmonious in sound and yet be filled with emptiness. If it does not spring from a love relationship with Jesus, it easily becomes something done by rote.

Such activities by themselves bring no enjoyment to God. However, when they are done through the life of His Son, it is a totally different matter. When Christ Himself is operative through His people, then the Father's pleasure is being fulfilled in the earth! He has purposed to corporately reveal His Son to the world. Anything less will not satisfy Him.

We look at the condition of the Church with all her divisions. People seek recognition through their ministries instead of serving. We see pride apparent in some, and realize how far we have yet to go in attaining what God has planned. The Body of Christ today is small, weak, divided and altogether unlovely when compared with her Head, the Lord Jesus. He is perfect in character and function. There is no need for Him to improve.

> "...but speaking the truth in love, we are to grow up in all aspects into Him, who is the head, even Christ..." (Eph. 4:15)

Christ's body must become a normal, functioning body that expresses the Head. When a human body does not respond to the impulses of the mind, that is deformity. The Church is in this condition. Together we must grow up into Him, the Head. We must mature into a visible expression of head and body. There will be a mature body (a corporate man) at Jesus' return.

"...until we all attain to...a mature man..." (Eph. 4:13)

If Jesus were to return for the Body of Christ in its present condition, Head and body would not be a picture of wholeness. There would be a well-formed Head with an emaciated body. This would certainly not reflect what God has purposed from eternity. God intends to bring forth a full-grown corporate man headed up by His Son. There is a stature that belongs to the fullness of Christ, and we must not settle for less (Eph. 4:13). What is the fullness of Christ? It is His body (Eph. 1:23). If we fail to understand this, the book of Ephesians will not make sense. A major emphasis of Paul in this epistle is the Church in all her glory (Eph. 5:27)! The heart of God longs for this. Many have not understood His heart and so they have misunderstood His activities in the earth. He is preparing a bride for His Son. He is building a house in which He will dwell forever. He is bringing to maturity a corporate man to reflect the mind of Christ in our generation.

All of these analogies picture God's good pleasure, which He purposed in Christ. His good pleasure is found in His Son. Thus His command to us is indisputable. We must live and abide in the Son, even as He lived in union with His

Father. As Jesus found His life in the Father, we are to find our life in the Son. Fruitfulness comes from abiding in Him (Jn. 15:5). God is looking for the fruit of His own life in the earth! He is not looking for "our best shot" (our best attempt at righteousness, ministry, winning the lost, building a successful church, etc.). He is simply looking for the life of His Son and for the fruit springing from that life. All other results testify of the ingenuity and strength of man in which God takes no delight.

God's people must recognize that apart from Him we can do nothing (Jn. 15:5), even as Jesus recognized that apart from His Father He could do nothing (Jn. 5:19). Then the Father will have the same gratification in us that He had in the Son! The Father saw *Himself* expressed in the earth through His Son (Jn. 14:9) and He was well pleased. Today He looks for no less than His Son to be expressed through His people. If we would bring pleasure to the heart of God, then we need to rely completely on the Holy Spirit, who has been sent to reveal Jesus in our midst.

## Chapter 13

# A View to an Administration

"...with a view to an administration suitable to the fulness of the times, that is, the summing up of all things in Christ, things in the heavens and things upon the earth." (Eph. 1:10)

God intends to establish an administration suitable to the fullness of the times (when time has come "to the full"). The word "administration" is the English translation of the Greek word OIKONOMIA from which we get the word "economy." OIKONOMIA is derived from two Greek words, OIKOS, which means "house" and NOMOS, meaning "law." So OIKONOMIA could be translated either as "economy," "administration" or "the law (management) of a house." Clearly this word expresses the concept of governmental oversight. God intends for the universe to be governed properly and He is moving in the Church to that end. In order to achieve this goal, He is first establishing order in His house, for judgment must begin there.

This is not to suggest that God is not governing the

universe properly already. Obviously He is. However, He must come to have first place in *everything,* including the hearts of His people (Col. 1:18). As a result of satan's rebellion and Adam's fall, disorder has come into God's universe and sin's effects are seen everywhere. Out of this chaos and disorder, God is moving to establish an "economy," an administration that will be suitable when time is completed. What God is doing in the earth now has eternal consequences. How *we respond* to what He is doing will have eternal consequences *for us!* What is at issue is not simply whether I will go to heaven or not. What faces me as a Christian is the question of *where I belong in His economy.*

Some Christians believe heaven will be the solution to all their problems. They think, "When I die and go to heaven, I will have total victory over sin." The problem with such thinking is that it reflects more confidence in *our* death and resurrection than in Christ's! Yet the basis for a victorious walk in the Christian faith is not found in the future. The foundation for victory is in the past! I have been baptized into *His* death and resurrection and so I am now able to walk as a new creature in Him! Heaven centeredness is not the answer; Jesus centeredness is. It is obviously not wrong to talk about going to heaven. Jesus did. However, He spoke only sparingly about going to heaven and a great deal about going to *the Father!* Jesus was Father centered! Heaven as a place did not dominate His thinking; the One who dwelt there did. Jesus was going to Some*one,* not to some*place!* If we are more concerned with going to heaven as a place, rather than to Him who dwells there, our priorities need to be adjusted.

God wants a heavenly people on the earth. This requires

us to be filled with the One who dwells in heaven! It is His presence that makes such a people. Talking about heaven is a poor substitute for a heavenly reality permeating our lives. A people filled with His presence is key to His plan of establishing an economy "...suitable to the fullness of the times..." His objective is not simply to get man (who was made out of the earth) into heaven, but to bring heaven and the order of heaven down to the earth and into earthen vessels. The incarnation involved God stepping down from heaven and *becoming* an earthen vessel. For the first time in history, the reality and order of heaven was found in a single individual. He was able to say, "...the Kingdom of God is in your midst." (Luke 17:21) Men were able to see God's economy, government and order perfectly expressed in one Man! Prior to His appearing on the scene, the house of God on earth was made up of natural material, with its order maintained and managed through the Law. God's intent today is that His house of "living stones" be marked by the order found in the foundation stone, the Lord Jesus Christ.

One of the major themes of the Old Testament is the house of the Lord. After the destruction of Solomon's temple, God promised through the prophet Haggai that the glory of the latter house (the rebuilt temple) would be greater than the former. Yet there is no Old Testament record of the cloud of God's glory entering the rebuilt temple! Notice, God did not promise the latter *house* would be greater than the former, but that the *glory* of the latter house would surpass the former. The glory of the former house (Solomon's temple) was God manifest in a cloud. The glory of the rebuilt house was God manifest in the flesh! When Jesus of Nazareth came into that temple, the Glory of Israel was manifest there! However, multitudes missed it when "the Glory" walked in. And multitudes missed it when He walked out.

> "O Jerusalem, Jerusalem, who kills the prophets and stones those who are sent to her! How often I wanted to gather your children together, the way a hen gathers her chicks under her wings, and you were unwilling. Behold, your house is being left to you desolate! For I say to you, from now on you shall not see Me until you say, 'Blessed is He who comes in the name of the Lord!' " (Matt. 23:37-39)

Notice Jesus' use of the word, "your." It was "their" house now. It was no longer His. Notice also His use of the word "being." Their house was *being* left desolate. Jesus spoke these words *as He was walking out!* The glory of God was departing! This was the most critical point in Israel's history and yet most people failed to recognize its significance.

What did He mean when He said they would no longer see Him until they could say, "Blessed is He who comes in the name of the Lord"? Did they not see Him a few days later hanging on the cross? Obviously they did. The context makes it clear that Jesus was not referring to His physical person. He was speaking as the Glory of Israel! They would see Him, but not with spiritual insight. They would no longer behold the glory of God. A few months later, as recorded in the second chapter of Acts, three thousand Jewish people in response to Peter's sermon, repented and in effect said, "Blessed is He who comes in the name of the Lord." They received Peter, who had come in Jesus' name, and in so doing they received their Messiah. Suddenly, they saw the Glory of Israel coming into His temple. God's temple (His people) was filled with His presence. Today His glory is in His house and we are able to behold that glory.

God plans to establish an OIKONOMIA (the law of a house) suitable to the fullness of the times. God governed His Old Testament house through Old Testament laws. He is governing the New Testament house by His indwelling presence through the Spirit. The order of God is established by His life, His indwelling presence. It will not be established by well-meaning men, trying in their own strength to bring structure to God's people! *He Himself is the law of His house.* As we submit to Him, we will find harmony in the horizontal realm (our relationship with our brethren). This will be a reflection of the harmony we have with Him. The reason disorder exists in the universe is because people are "out of tune" with their Creator. Disorder exists in the Church for the same reason!

We have believed that order was implicit in a well-defined and well-functioning group of people. We thought good programs, a competent administrative staff, and a firm voice of control at the top were necessary. While these can certainly appear very successful, the order of God involves each of His people walking and functioning in the Spirit together. *Corporate harmony is the product of individual obedience.*

"...the whole body, being fitted and held together by that which every joint supplies, according to the proper working of each individual part, causes the growth of the body for the building up of itself in love." (Eph. 4:16)

As each member functions properly, the Body of Christ builds itself up, and thereby comes into the order of God.

Either His order springs from those having good administrative abilities, or it springs from many people offering themselves freely to the will of God. The order of God is precisely that; it is the order *of God!* Springing from *His life*, it fills His whole body. Leadership does not order the house of God. Rather leaders are to *oversee* the process as *He* orders His house, through the ministry of His life!

God is estabishing the management of His house that will be suitable to the fullness of the times. That is where He is going in these days. Let's go with Him.

# Chapter 14

# We Were Made a Heritage

"...in whom also we were made a heritage, having been foreordained according to the purpose of him who worketh all things after the counsel of his will." (Eph. 1:11 ASV)

In Christ, we have become God's inheritance.

"I pray that the eyes of your heart may be enlightened, so that you may know what is the hope of His calling, what are the riches of the glory of His inheritance in the saints." (Eph. 1:18 NASB)

The major emphasis of Scripture is "the purpose of God," that is, what He stands to receive as a consequence of His redemptive dealings with His people. Man-centeredness, however, dominates much of the Church's thinking. Most preaching today concerns what man receives from God, whereas what God is doing and why—His goals—should be the center of our attention. *Eternity will not be filled with man and his need, but with God and His glory!* The primary issue of the ages is not man, his fall and his redemption, but what God is accomplishing for His own Name's sake. Truly, our benefits of salvation are great, but the purposes of God are greater. We tend to focus on symptoms rather than causes, to see things from our finite perspective. However, God wants us to see with spiritual insight into the eternal realm. It will only be those with an eternal perspective who will really grasp God's intentions as He brings this age to an end. These, like Paul, will "make the connection," "tap into" the presence of God and grasp the glory of His eternal purpose.

> "For from Him and through Him and to Him are all things. To Him be the glory forever. Amen." (Rom. 11:36)

This verse indicates the all inclusiveness of Jesus. "From Him" means He is the Author of the purposes of God. "Through Him" means He became the channel to accomplish them. "To Him" means He is the goal and ultimate objective of those purposes! We are baptized into Him and His purposes. Instead of simply endeavoring to include God in our lives, we must recognize that God has offered to include us in His! This may only seem a perspective, but a proper perspective is crucial in order to participate fully in the purposes of God. He has promised to meet our needs, because of His great love. However, we should not concentrate on how to get God to respond to our needs, nor even those of people around us. Rather we must learn to see clearly what He is doing and cooperate with Him. More is accomplished when we cooperate with God and focus on Him than when we focus on meeting the needs we see around us. Our interpretation of a situation is always limited; His is infinite. We often feel frustrated when He does not respond to our prayers the way we would like. However, God's word to us is, "Stop trying to bring Me down to your level of understanding. Instead, be filled with My life and I will bring you to new heights in Me and give you insights you never would have conceived of on your own."

God's concern is to get people with finite minds to grasp infinite truth. We are called to understand what is beyond our ability to comprehend. Then we are called to preach this infinite wisdom of God! One might say, "That is impossible!" Right! That is the point! Christianity is miraculous by nature. We are called to participate in the impossible. We are not called to simply take Christian truth and educate people's minds. We must stand in the presence of the Almighty and receive insight into His heart and declare with confidence what He reveals. This principle is foundational for a proper building of Christ's Church.

> "And Simon Peter answered and said, 'Thou art the Christ, the Son of the living God.' And Jesus answered and said to him, 'Blessed are you Simon Barjona, because flesh and blood did not reveal this to you, but My Father who is in heaven. And I also say to you that you are Peter, and upon this rock I will build My church; and the gates of Hades shall not overpower it.' " (Matt. 16:16-18)

Jesus did not say Peter was blessed because he understood this great truth. Rather, he was blessed because of *how he received this truth!* It had come through a direct revelation from the Father! Peter had not received this from another man. God Himself had "taken Peter aside" and unveiled an eternal insight to him. In light of this, Jesus began unfolding His plans to build a people together that hell would fail to defeat. Peter had just graduated! His name was changed. Jesus had previously said,

> "You are Simon the son of John; you shall be called Cephas (which translated means Peter)." (Jn. 1:42)

In Scripture, a man's name often has significance. In a particular context of Scripture, the meaning of a name gives insight into how God would use that person. Simon means, "to hear with acceptance." Peter means, "a stone." In other words, as Peter endeavored to walk with God and learn to hear and obey His voice, God would make him a living stone in His house. When Peter declared Jesus' messiahship, Jesus knew Peter had come into a new dimension in God. Now He could say, "You were Simon, but now you *are Peter.*" When Jesus saw the *personal revelation* that God had blessed Peter with, He in effect said, *"This* is the rock I will build My church on." The foundation of the Church is not the truth that Jesus is the Messiah. It is the *personal, God-given revelation in each individual's heart that Jesus is that person's Messiah.*

When God reveals His Son as Savior and Messiah to one who hears with faith (i.e., he repents and receives God's solution for his sin), that person becomes a living stone in the house of God. God will then build him into His house in such a way that hell itself cannot prevail against him.

Attacks from hell cannot shake one who stands firmly on the personal revelation from heaven concerning who Jesus is! He may stumble from time to time such as Peter did, but there will be such a heavenly reality in his heart that the forces of hell will not be able to quench it. The "gates of hades" are presently trying to destroy the Church of Jesus Christ. The word "gates" in Scripture refers to a place of wisdom, power, judgment, strategy, etc. Men of reputation in a city sat as elders and transacted important affairs in the gates of their city (Ruth 4:1-11, Prov. 31:23). When Jesus said the gates of hades would not prevail against His Church, He basically said the greatest human or demonic strategies that hell has to throw against us will not succeed! However, overcoming the forces of hell is based on our receiving a first-hand revelation from heaven concerning the Lord Jesus Christ! The Rock that the Church is built on is Jesus revealed by God to the hearts of men.

> "For I would have you know, brethren, that the gospel which was preached by me is not according to man. For I neither received it from man, nor was I taught it, but I received it through a revelation of Jesus Christ." (Gal. 1:11,12)

God uses His people to preach the gospel of the kingdom. However, that gospel will just be head-knowledge to the hearer until God Himself reveals His Son to that person's heart. Until revelation comes, that individual is not yet born into the Church. Information alone does not produce true Christianity; the impartation of His life is required. The spiritual birth is both miraculous and necessary! If our birth is miraculous, so also should be our walk and ministry! So often we start in the Spirit but we do not *continue* in the Spirit.

"If we live by the Spirit, let us also walk by the Spirit." (Gal. 5:25)

What God has begun in us He will complete as we walk in a life-style that is in harmony with the Spirit we have received. He has not brought us to birth just so we can go to heaven someday. He has given us His life so that the reality of heaven might be tasted and expressed here in the earth! He is doing something for Himself, for His own Name's sake in this present age.

Over the years Christians have focused primarily on what God has done *for* them and then have failed to see what God intends to do *through* them *for Himself.* As a result, we have failed to understand the glory of the riches of *His* inheritance in the saints! What does He plan to achieve? He will have a house to dwell in forever; He will have a bride to rule the universe with Him, side by side; He will crush the power of hell itself through a people made from the dust of the ground and infused with the eternal power of His own life. There will arise a God ordained order that will sustain His universe. Today, there is emerging a heavenly people through whom He is presently waging war as He moves to bring all things under His feet! Let us be counted among that people. Let us so abide in Him that He finds His heart fulfilled in us even as we find our hearts fulfilled in Him.

# Chapter 15

# We Were Made a Heritage II

"...in whom also we were made a heritage, having been foreordained according to the purpose of him who worketh all things after the counsel of his will." (Eph. 1:11 ASV)

As God's people, we are His inheritance; therefore, no longer can we live for ourselves. We have become His unique treasure among all the people on the earth. In the Old Testament, Israel was God's inheritance among the nations.

"And Moses went up to God, and the Lord called to him from the mountain, saying, 'Thus you shall say to the house of Jacob and tell the sons of Israel: You yourselves have seen what I did to the Egyptians, and how I bore you on eagles' wings, and brought you to *Myself.*' " (Ex. 19:3,4, emphasis mine)

We generally view the exodus as Israel's deliverance *from Egypt.* However, God's perspective was that they were brought *to Him.* The Israelites were not simply leaving a land of bondage, they were going *to the Lord.* They succeeded in coming out of Egypt, but by and large, they failed in going to Him.

Similarly in the Church today, much is preached concerning how God sent a Deliverer (the Lord Jesus) to lead us out from the bondage of the world (our Egypt) and unto Himself. However, like Israel, we have not come unto Him as we should. We have been satisfied to see our deliverance from something, but we have not understood our call *to Someone!* It is only through giving ourselves to Him that we fully establish our identity as God's people. To be His people means we belong to Him, not to ourselves; we are His inheritance.

Israel's primary failure was not realizing they were God's inheritance. The Church's primary failure has been the same. We have testified that He is our God, that He is always with us and will never leave nor forsake us. While this is true, the other side of the coin is that we are His. We belong totally to Him!

"I am my beloved's and my beloved is mine." (Songs 6:3)

We focus on half of the message in our preaching! Belonging to Him means we have forfeited the right to govern our own lives! He has the right to adjust anything in us that is not comfortable to Him, that does not suit His taste. For example, if your bed was uncomfortable to sleep in, you would think nothing of either getting rid of it or adjusting it. Or if you liked a particular color or decor, you would feel free to do whatever had to be done to make your home more suitable to yourself. God has paid a high price for us; we are His house and He has come to dwell in what is His. Therefore, He has the right to "repaint, repaper, repair," to make whatever changes that would best reflect His character and His will. The degree that we submit to Him as He "restores" us, shows that we understand what it means to be His inheritance.

> "Now then, if you will indeed obey My voice and keep My covenant, then you shall be My own possession [or 'My special treasure'] among all the peoples, for all the earth is mine." (Ex. 19:5)

In effect, God said to Israel, "Listen, I own everything including you. If you desire to *reflect that ownership,* then walk in obedience to Me and you will be unique among all the peoples of the earth as My special treasure."

> "And you shall be to Me a kingdom of priests and a holy nation." (Ex. 19:6)

Our mission becomes defined for us once we understand our identity. For example, a quarterback on a football team understands his mission because he knows what position he plays. However, if he thinks he is a halfback, he will bring confusion on the field. God must reveal to us who we are, or else we will never get our mission right! First He tells us we are His. Then He says that if we will walk in the reality of that ownership ( in obedience), our identity will be established as *a kingdom of priests* and *a holy nation.* Unfortunately, Israel never became a kingdom of priests. God had to choose one of the tribes (Levi) from which to secure a priesthood to serve Him. They also never became a holy nation.

We see this failure throughout their history in the Old Testament. In neglecting to come to Him with all their hearts, they failed to recognize their true identity and thereby failed to accomplish their mission (to be a light to the nations).

What does it mean to be a kingdom of priests and a holy nation, for these terms obviously apply to the Church today (1 Pet. 2:9)?

*A kingdom of priests (or royal priesthood)* speaks of a people under a King, or of kingly lineage, all of who may come and stand in the presence of the Lord and minister to Him. The first priority of a priesthood, those separated for service, is to serve the one who has called them for service. To stand before a holy God requires that a priest meet His qualifications. When a people are more concerned with what others think of them, than with what God thinks of them, they fail to understand the call to priesthood. Much of what is done in Christendom appears impressive at first glance. But the question arises, "Why has the Church had so little lasting impact on the nations?" We want to take God with us out into the world. However, God's priority is that we understand we are His! Then armed with this insight and life-style, our ministry is to reflect to the world *what we are unto Him.* If we witness to unbelievers about the Lord while not offering ourselves to Him as a living sacrifice, then our words will have the hollow sound of religious jargon. We may express an accurate theology, but the reality of God's kingdom will be missing from our lives. Thus our words will carry no more weight than those of any other philosopher who has some new "truth" to propagate. The world does not need more words about God. It needs a people whose lives reflect the reality of a holy priesthood relationship with

God. We must become a functional priesthood. We must be that sacrifice which is offered as a sweet fragrance to the Lord if we are ever to impact the nations (Rom. 12:1)!

*A holy nation* has to do with our corporate identity in the world. Sadly, the Church today looks more like a feudal system than a unique nation. Within her are many little governments, systems, institutions and ministries. One would think God was confused! The truth that the Church is a holy people standing as one under a single government (Jesus as King) is certainly not evident to the world. It is even doubtful if the Church really believes it either! We talk about "our" church, "their" church (the folks that meet down the road), how many churches there are in our city, as though such a condition is normal. We have not grasped the reality of our identity and so have failed to become His holy nation! We have missed it as badly as Israel did! Consequently, we see the same two failures in the Lord's inheritance today as occurred in Israel.

*Clergy-laity separation.* Instead of the whole people of God standing in His presence, responsible to hear His voice, we have the clergy as a section of the Church singled out from the rest as special. In some groups they even dress differently to emphasize their religious station. This "special" group is expected to stand before the Lord on behalf of the others. However, a clergy-laity distinction, both in the Old and New Testaments, was never God's best! *His whole kingdom* is to be comprised of priests!

*Captivity.* Because we have failed to be a holy nation, like Israel, we have been carried off and scattered by our enemies. Satan has had a "field day." Not only has the Church been divided by selfishness, lust, greed, the desire to be seen as a great success in ministry, etc., but men have also separated themselves from one another because of disagreement over their concepts of biblical truth. In pursuit of doctrinal purity and failing to acknowledge their pride concerning doctrine, they are *forced* to keep at a distance from all who disagree with them. To embrace one who differed would undermine the whole basis for their separation. Such action would, in their view, bring "spiritual infection" upon themselves. Thus the result is *a bondage to their present divided condition.*

With such opportunities for the enemy to infiltrate and scatter God's inheritance, there has occurred a captivity of greater magnitude than the Babylonian captivity in the Old Testament! That first captivity involved the people being carried away physically. The consequences were obvious. However, the present captivity is spiritual and therefore many have not recognized it! However, like God's people in Nehemiah's day, we are living in a time of restoration. A prophetic trumpet is being sounded, bondages are being broken and a great regathering of God's people is beginning to occur. Remember, we are God's inheritance. He will show Himself mighty to restore to Himself those who are His!

# Chapter 16

# Predestined Acccording to His Purpose

> "...in whom also we were made a heritage, having been foreordained according to the purpose of him who worketh all things after the counsel of his will." (Eph. 1:11 ASV)

Throughout history, the burden of prophetic ministry has been to call the people of God to return to Him with all of their hearts and to recognize themselves as His inheritance. Whenever they have responded to that call, the result has invariably been new demonstrations of the power of God in the earth. Whenever His people have not responded, the result has been a perpetuation of religious formalism with many *words* about spiritual reality, but without the *substance* of that reality expressed in their lives. Such a caricature of His life cannot impact the nations; only a Church that fully embraces her calling will do so. Only a Church that understands the implications of being His inheritance, that she belongs totally to Him, will become in practice what God has called her to be.

What then does it mean to be God's inheritance? First, God predestined a people for Himself. He knew who they were because of His foreknowledge of their response to the gospel. He then set about to produce in them the qualities that would mark them as His possession. This required that He become a man, take the sins of the world upon Himself, die, be raised from the dead and finally pour His Spirit upon those who believe in Him. In turn, His Spirit within them would seek to express His Lordship and ownership; not in the future only, but now, and not from some place far off (heaven) but from right here on earth! However, after we receive the Spirit, the task ahead of Him in establishing us as His inheritance is immense. It is nothing less than working out today what He has seen from eternity *causing His people to reflect His ownership!* Both the Scriptures and Church history reveal the dealings of God with man to accomplish this miracle. At issue is not whether God's sovereign foreknowledge is greater than man's will (a question scholars like to debate). The question is: Will His people cooperate with Him in what He determines to do? Are we in harmony with His stated purpose to put all enemies under His feet? Or do our lives reflect man-centeredness and self-centeredness, even when our doctrine is theologically sound?

Christian leadership usually strives for theological accuracy. While this is important, Christ's Lordship is demonstrated more by godly individual and corporate life-styles than it is in accurate religious dogma. What we preach must be backed up by holy lives. The intellectual tenets of the Kingdom of God have very practical implications.

One such tenet is,

"the righteous man shall live by faith." (Rom. 1:17)

Some Christian teachers emphasize that the righteous shall *get* (receive) by faith. Obviously it *is* by faith that we receive anything from God, whether it is salvation, physical healing, or any good gift. However, the emphasis of Scripture is not *getting from* God, but *living for* God! Living for Him is more than merely existing. Living for Him by faith involves an entire life-style that reflects the faith in our hearts.

This is what chapter eleven of Hebrews is all about. It contains the testimonies of individuals who believed in God, lived for Him and made their mark in history. They walked out the reality of His ownership of them. They were God's inheritance in the earth! None began in perfect obedience to the Lord; imperfections were found in everyone. However, because of God's sovereignty and His great love for them, He worked all things in their lives after the counsel of His will. As a result, the outworking of His eternal plan in the lives of believing men and women is what we find recorded in Scripture. This should encourage us to recognize that He acts the same way today! One problem is that we esteem ourselves as insignificant and unimportant compared to the great political and economic leaders of our day. We see men jetting around the world, influencing nations and we begin to question the Church's significance in the world. When we consider Abraham, King David and other mighty men of Scripture it also causes us to think that we might be un-important in *God's* sight as well! "I could never be like those spiritual giants," we seem to say. At such a time of dis-couragement, Paul's words are so enlightening!

"In Him also we were made a heritage having been predestined according to His purpose who works all things after the counsel of His will." (Eph. 1:1 NASB and ASV)

Suddenly, by revelation, we get a glimpse of the way God Himself sees us. His eternal purposes involve *us!* He is at work in and through us in our generation, just like He was in the lives of the great men and women of the Bible. Just as they made their mark in history, so also what God is doing in you and me is intended to be of eternal consequence! The world may not understand or recognize God's activities in us. We may never be considered a success by the standards of society. However, something known in the heart of God from eternity is being expressed through our lives today!

God *is* at work in His inheritance. The love and tender care with which He deals in our lives is often misunderstood by even His own children. However, if we could see with His eyes, we would understand that He truly *does* work all things after the counsel of His will. To *recognize* that He is moving in our lives as He was moving in Abraham's and others' brings us to the place of decision. Our lives *will* begin to reflect the faith in our hearts and as a result we will speak with confidence concerning His commitment to us. As Christians, we should hold our heads high. We have been chosen by God from eternity. We are His inheritance in the earth, and He is at work in us so that we might increasingly reflect His ownership. This is what it means to be a witness for Him. The more whole-heartedly we yield to Him, the more conscious we will be of our place in His purpose. Thus we can know that He is working all things after the counsel of His will in our lives...

"...to the end that we who were the first to hope in Christ should *be* to the praise of His glory." (Eph. 1:12, emphasis mine)

May we submit readily and joyfully as the Lord brings us forth in His likeness, that we might *be* an inspiration of praise to Him from all creation. May He be glorified for what His grace accomplishes in us!

# Chapter 17

# The Counsel of His Will

"In Him also we were made a heritage, having been predestined according to His purpose who works all things after the counsel of His will." (Eph. 1:11 NASB and ASV)

We are God's inheritance, not because of strategic planning and human effort on our part, but because He has purposed it. He works *all* things after the counsel of His will. When the Lord considers our needs, He does not experiment to find the best solution. He acts according to what He purposed to do before time began. God does not make up a plan of action for us as He goes along. He works out in time what He has known from eternity. God never reacts!

It is fortunate for us that the Lord does not function in our lives in the same manner men operate governments and businesses. Since men do not know the future, they respond to events as they occur. If inflation begins to accelerate, businesses change their strategy accordingly. If a recession

looms on the horizon, then another plan has to be imple-
mented. When a foreign power is overthrown, our government's foreign policy has to be suddenly adjusted. Men *must*
react when the unforeseen happens, because no one can
possibly know all details of the future.

However, God does not operate this way. He does not
*react,* He acts! God is the Divine Initiator. The universe did
not decide to exist! God made a decision and, by speaking,
He created that which declares His glory. Man, the highest
order of this creation, was formed from the dust of the
ground and became a living being as God breathed life into
him. When He created Adam, the Lord saw all who would
eventually come forth from him. Every man has had Adam
as his father—every man except One, of course. The last
Adam, Jesus, was different than any other born on the earth.
This One was not given life from a fallen nature. He was
brought forth in holiness. He is the first-born. When Adam
fell, all of creation fell with him. In contrast, when Jesus
rose from the dead and ascended to the Father, all those
who would believe in Him rose, ascended and today are
seated with Him by faith in heavenly places.

God knew that Adam would fall even before He created
him. Sin did not catch Him unaware. Calvary was not a
*re*action by the Lord to something that had taken Him by
surprise. It was an action, the cost of which He had counted
from eternity. God does not "roll with the punches"; He foreknows them! If Calvary was an afterthought in response to
satan's initiative, then redemption is a reaction by God rather
than part of His eternal plan. Such thinking is an inappropri-
ate and limited perspective of God and His purposes.

Satan is bigger in the thoughts of many Christians than he is in reality. To their minds, God's war with satan is between two spiritual beings who are almost equal, and the outcome is not totally clear. Nothing could be further from the truth! God is so much greater than satan, that it is like comparing a man to a flea! However, even that is not an accurate analogy because a man is finite and God is infinite. Perhaps a thousand men versus one flea would be more appropriate. Even then, a thousand men are still finite. You simply cannot compare the infinite God with a finite created being. Satan is simply not in the same class as God! I am not minimizing the reality of satan's power, but I am exalting *God's* power to illustrate the nature of the call He extends to us. We are not called by God as an afterthought on His part. We are not saved and filled with the Spirit because He had no other options left once satan appeared to have messed up His original plan. No, we *are* God's original plan! Our destiny is a *pre*destiny! Our destiny is eternal in its inception and eternal in its consummation. We, who are living today in relationship with God, have tasted the future and have been brought into participation with Him in eternity. It is no wonder satan opposes us so much. He endeavors to keep us unaware of who we are in Christ and unaware of the significance of our calling!

As we come to grips with our place in the eternal purposes of God, we will rise above satan's deceptions. Satan may come masquerading as God to put thoughts in our minds, such as, "If I had known what you were *really* like, I never would have chosen you." If we accept this as God's voice, we will doubt His commitment to us. We will conclude that His plan for our lives is not very important to *Him,* because we now believe *we* are unimportant to Him. As a result, His plan will be unimportant to us and we will not give ourselves to His call. Many people do not pursue the will of God simply because they do not consider *themselves* important to Him. If we realized how precious we are in His eyes, we would recognize how excellent His will is for our lives and we would run after it with all our might! We have been loved from eternity! We have been chosen by One who foreknew *every* flaw we would have and every mistake we would make. And He died gladly that we might have forgiveness for our sins and be enabled to participate in His purpose—that which is good, acceptable and perfect.

"I urge you therefore, brethren, by the mercies of God, to present your bodies a living and holy sacrifice, acceptable to God, which is your spiritual service of worship. And do not be conformed to this world, but be transformed by the renewing of your mind, that you may prove what the will of God is, that which is good and acceptable and perfect." (Rom. 12:1,2)

The word "transformed" is the Greek word META-MORPHOO from which we get the English word "metamorphosis," that amazing process by which a caterpillar becomes a beautiful butterfly. As we submit to God's dealings in our lives, He begins to change our outlook on Him, life, people and ourselves. As a result, we soon realize that His will is good, acceptable and perfect. To prove His will means to try, test and examine the consequences of obeying Him in our decisions. God wants us to *prove* that His will is perfect. The greatest testimony occurs when a people, because of their obedience to Him, leave behind the "caterpillar" attributes of fear, self-centeredness, jealousy and other attitudes of the flesh and emerge with a genuine love for God and others. Sometimes we are more conscious of appearing like a caterpillar than a butterfly. However, the butterfly life within (the life of God) draws us continually to Him, that He may renew our minds until the metamorphic process is effectively worked out in us.

What God is doing in His people and in the earth is according to the counsel of His own will, which is perfect. When a decision has to be made concerning us, He stops and asks, "What did I determine to do from all eternity with this one?" He then takes counsel from His own eternal perspective, and that which is good, acceptable and perfect is effected for us. Then as we walk in harmony with Him, we *prove to ourselves* the goodness and perfection of His will. As a result, we become living proof to others of this truth.

May God continue to cause us to see with ever greater clarity the perfection of His plan for our lives. May we give ourselves with total abandon to the pursuit of Him and what He has purposed to do from eternity.

# Chapter 18

# We Who Were the First...
# You Also

"Also we were made a heritage, having been predestined according to His purpose who works all things after the counsel of His will, to the end that *we who were the first* to hope in Christ should be to the praise of His glory. In Him, *you also,* after listening to the message of truth, the gospel of your salvation—having also believed, you were sealed in Him with the Holy Spirit of promise." (Eph. 1:11-13 NASB and ASV, emphasis mine)

Until the revelation of the Messiah, the Jewish people lived under a "tutor" (the Law). Once saving faith in the person of Christ was opened up to them, this became the way of righteousness to be proclaimed to *all* men. Thus God's promise that *all* nations would be blessed through Abraham could now be fulfilled as these first century Jews "who were the first to hope in Christ" began to walk, like Abraham, in a faith relationship with God.

"But before faith came, we were kept in custody under the Law, being shut up to the faith which was later to be revealed. Therefore the Law has become our tutor to lead us to Christ, that we may be justified by faith. But now that faith has come, we are no longer under a tutor. For you are all sons of God through faith in Christ Jesus. For all of you who were baptized into Christ have clothed yourselves with Christ. There is neither Jew nor Greek, there is neither slave nor free man, there is neither male nor female; for you are all one in Christ Jesus." (Gal. 3:23-28)

Through faith in Christ, the covenant nation of God is now comprised 1) of men and women, 2) from all races, and 3) from all social and cultural spheres. However, when Paul says, "There is neither Jew nor Greek," he is not ignoring racial differences; he is standing against any form of discrimination. Obviously there were men and women in the Church of Paul's day, as well as slaves and free men. It was simply that there was to be no partiality around these distinctions in the Church, for God shows no partiality (Eph. 6:9).

Nonetheless, neither does the Bible teach that God's people are to be uniformly alike. The great diversity in the Body of Christ (gifting, personality, economic status) contributes an effectiveness in reaching all the different strata of society. God's people need to present the gospel of the kingdom right where they are. For example:

"Let all who are under the yoke as slaves regard their own masters as worthy of all honor so that the name of

God and our doctrine may not be spoken against. And let those who have believers as their masters not be disrespectful to them because they are brethren, but let them serve them all the more, because those who partake of the benefit are believers and beloved." (1 Tim. 6:1,2)

Believing slaves and masters met together in the same local churches in Paul's day. This is an unmistakable example of economic disparity. Yet while economically and socially unequal, masters and slaves stood before the Lord as equal; they were to treat each other as brothers. God had the right to choose either one to speak through when addressing His Church. If slave and master respected the distinctions between them (the slave not using his equality before the Lord to justify laziness on the job and the master not abusing his position as owner to suppress the slave from serving God), then mutual respect would bring true equality in the Church without obliterating the distinctions. Obviously society would not treat them as equals. However, the issue is not society. The issue is how believers are to conduct themselves in fellowship as a *testimony* to society of God's character.

In Christ there is neither male nor female; yet men need to be men, and women need to be women. It may appear that equality of the sexes can only be attained by diminishing the distinctions. However, equality is not synonymous with being alike; equality is *mutual respect regardless of distinctions!* Furthermore, there are not only different physical and emotional attributes in men and women, but also differences in how they function in the Church. However, this does not negate their equality or their worth; it expresses their diversity! The strength of the Body of Christ lies in each individual finding his or her unique place of spiritual service. Equality is not a matter of having the same function, but of being purchased for the same price, the blood of Jesus! My right hand and left foot do not have the same function, but both are equally important to me. Thus, recognizing the distinction between male and female is not only good and proper, but necessary. However, partiality is wrong. Society must *not* see in the Church either chauvinism or extreme feminism.

"For he is not a Jew who is one outwardly; neither is circumcision that which is outward in the flesh. But he is a Jew who is one inwardly; and circumcision is that which is of the heart, by the Spirit, not by the letter; and his praise is not from men, but from God." (Rom. 2:28,29)

When one emphasizes his identity in externals such as race or traditional religious rites (such as circumcision), any praise he receives in these areas will only come from men who also value such things. Those of common race and/or religion will be greatly pleased with him and speak of how he is now *one of them.* However, Paul states that one who has embraced God's true covenant has been circumcised in his *heart* by the Spirit of God. The Lord, seeing his heart, will then honor him as a participant in the covenant. Thus a Spirit-filled Gentile is, in fact, a true Jew in God's sight! While a Jew who rejects his Messiah is outside the covenant community, even though he might be physically circumcised.

When the Scriptures do make a distinction between Jews and Gentiles, it is not done to show partiality, but to unveil a significant truth. While preaching to Jewish people, Peter said:

"...Repent therefore and return, that your sins may be wiped away, in order that times of refreshing may come from the presence of the Lord; and that He may send Jesus, the Christ appointed for *you.*" (Acts 3:19,20, emphasis mine)

He goes on to quote Moses in the next part of his message and then concludes with,

"It is you who are the sons of the prophets, and of the covenant which God made with your fathers, saying to Abraham, 'And in your seed all the families of the earth shall be blessed.' For you *first,* God raised up His servant, and sent Him to bless *you* by turning every one of you from your wicked ways." (Acts 3:25,26, emphasis mine)

The gospel, by its very nature, is to the Jew first and then to the Gentile, but always without partiality. Jesus was the Christ appointed for *them;* He had been promised to them! In these promises, God made it clear that He intended to reach beyond them to the nations. In Abraham, all the families of the earth would be blessed. We Gentile believers have been brought into the fulfillment of promises made to *Jews* thousands of years ago. We who were far off from the covenants of promise have been brought near by the blood of Jesus (Eph. 2:12,13). Now we are partakers together with all who believe on His Name, both Jew and Gentile.

May we not be afraid of economic, sexual and racial distinctions in the Body of Christ. Let us honor each other and find great strength in the diversity that is to be the hallmark of the Lord's Church.

# Chapter 19

# We Who Were the First to Hope in Christ

"...to the end that we who were the first to hope in Christ should be to the praise of His glory." (Eph. 1:12)

Jesus was born a Jew, a descendant of Abraham and David. He was sent by His Father to be their promised Messiah, yet as a nation they failed to recognize Him. Obviously, He *could* have come in such dynamic majesty that the world would have immediately embraced Him. But God's ways are not our ways. Jesus came in lowliness and humility, and humanity did not perceive this to be a measure of greatness, as something worthy of acceptance. However, God was not surprised when the nation of Israel rejected His Son; He already foreknew it. He also foreknew that a company of people within Israel would turn and receive Jesus as their destined Messiah. God's intention was that this faithful remnant *be* to the praise of His glory.

"He was in the world, and the world was made through Him, and the world did not know Him. He came to His own, and those who were His own did not receive Him. But as many as received Him, to them He gave the right to become children of God, even to those who believe in His name, who were born not of blood, nor of the will of the flesh, nor of the will of man, but of God." (Jn. 1:10-13)

This Jewish remnant who chose to receive Jesus as their Messiah received the right to become children (Greek "born ones") of God. The way was opened for them to come into a Father-child relationship with God through a birth from above. Their birth was not based on the will of man, the desires of the flesh, or what blood (natural lineage) they were from, but on the will of God. The basis for one's entrance into the family of God, whether Jew or Gentile, is totally supernatural. This was contrary to what most Israelites expected. Generally, the Jewish people considered themselves safe in the purposes of God because they were of the "seed of Abraham." After all, the promises had been made to Abraham and his descendants. All the families of the earth would be blessed through him. So the attitude of many, undoubtedly was, "How can we miss it? God needs us to fulfill His promises to Abraham." However, God sent John the Baptist to strike a blow at such thinking.

"Therefore bring forth fruit in keeping with repentance; and do not suppose that you can say to yourselves, 'We have Abraham for our father'; for I say to you, that God is able from these stones to raise up children to Abraham. And the axe is already laid at the root of the trees; every tree therefore that does not bear good fruit is cut down and thrown into the fire." (Matt. 3:8-10)

John warned them not to find security in being natural descendants of Abraham. Only God Himself is the true refuge for His people. If He desired to, God could have taken stones lying on the ground and created a people that would obey Him. However, His heart longed to see the fruit of repentant hearts. God's people were the trees of the Lord, planted by God Himself (Ps. 92:12-15, Isa. 61:3, Matt. 7:16-20). The axe was laid to the root of the concept that nationality was the basis of God's choice. In effect, John said, "No longer say you are descendants of Abraham. Stop relying on that for your identity. Cease thinking you are secure in the purposes of God simply because you can trace your lineage back to him. But turn your hearts in sincerity to the living God and bear the spiritual fruit *He* seeks. From this day on He has cut away the right for you to lean on your Abrahamic descent. If you do not bring forth godly fruit, the fires of judgment await you." Needless to say, John immediately became unpopular with the religious leaders of his day. Not only because he preached repentance, but because he prophesied against that in which they found their identity and security.

What John confronted in the Pharisees is the same basic problem that God's prophets have faced in every generation. The burden of prophets has always been to turn God's people back to Him with a whole heart and reveal Him to be everything they need. Today, many in the Church find security and identity in being Baptists or Methodists or Catholics. Some find it in being non-denominational. Still others gravitate around words like Charismatic, Evangelical or Fundamentalist. However, if we truly repent of any confidence in such identity, we will find a greater appreciation of our common root.

"...being rooted and grounded in *love* [Greek, AGAPE]." (Eph. 3:17, emphasis mine)

Once we recognize our common root (the *love* of God expressed from eternity in Jesus' death, burial, resurrection and ascension), *then* we will more clearly understand our unique identity as the people of God. Only then will we stop focusing on differences in one another. Only then will we stop seeing each other as the enemy, and start doing battle with *one* voice against the forces of darkness!

God foresaw a Jewish remnant, a company of people of the natural lineage of Abraham who would come forth to the praise of His glory. Peter, James, John, Paul and many other Jewish men and women were mightily used of God in the initial impact of the gospel in the earth. They were the remnant who expressed the praise of His glory; and what a powerful demonstration of His glory it was! Jews from every nation under heaven were in Jerusalem on the day of Pentecost as He poured out His Spirit and began a proclamation of the gospel. That Jewish remnant was His strike force! God intended that through them, the gospel would be taken to all nations. As is often the case though, *God's people did not understand His purpose in blessing them.* Many Jewish believers expected God simply to renew the nation of *Israel* by saving Jews and filling *only them* with the Holy Spirit. Thus, when Peter went to Cornelius' house and preached to the Gentiles there, the church leaders in Jerusalem became upset with him (Acts 11:1-3). But this contact was central in the purpose of God! The remnant was commissioned to take the good news of salvation to all men, to every nation.

God has always had a remnant people. Men like Jeremiah, Elijah and Daniel, were always to be found in Israel even when most of the nation was backsliding. Today, it is no different. As the Lord prepares the Church for His return, He is looking for that remnant, a people who love Him and who are rooted in Him. These are days of holy visitation. He is pouring His Spirit upon the Church today, just as He did on that Jewish remnant in the second chapter of Acts. However, as He restores the Church, extending the borders of His kingdom, we must understand His *purpose* in blessing us. He is not pouring out His Spirit on us so we can do what *we* want. He has a plan, a strategy. He is headed somewhere. It is so easy for His people to become stale, dry and corporately arthritic. When that happens, God begins to lay an axe to the root of whatever we find our security and identity in. He searches for those who will bear the fruit of repentance and follow Him with a whole heart. It is through such dealings that the Kingdom of God is extended. Let us be counted among God's remnant today, having our security and identity in Him.

# Chapter 20

# The Message of Truth

"In Him, you also, after listening to the message of truth, the gospel of your salvation—having also believed, you were sealed in Him with the Holy Spirit of promise." (Eph. 1:13)

With so many political, economic, scientific, religious and philosophical theories being propagated in our society, it is not always clear what is truth and what is error. Sometimes the issue can be so overwhelming that we find ourselves, like Pilate, asking,

"What is truth?" (Jn. 18:38)

When Pilate asked this question, he was facing the only man in history who claimed to *be* truth personified. Jesus never said He *had the facts,* He said He *was the truth.* What is the difference? Facts are simply a collection of accurate data. We can be led astray by facts. Scientists can collect a great quantity of data and yet come to a wrong *conclusion* concerning its significance. For example, while archae-ological study of fossils has not proven the theory of evolu-tion, many conclude that it has. Facts, by themselves, may or may not have moral significance. However, truth is the ultimate reality of the person and purpose of God; it is expressed in the gospel.

Jesus said He was the truth because He presented the reality of who God is to a fallen world in terms anyone could understand. When men came into contact with Christ, they touched something more than all the information they had accumulated concerning God. This One embodied all of that, and more. Jesus did not memorize all the scriptures concerning God and then express what He had read. *He was the message the Bible was written to reveal, the very Word of God made flesh!* However, many who studied the Scriptures found that Jesus did not fit their perception of God. They were more comfortable with their *interpretations* of what God was like, than with His reality in their midst! When they came into contact with God, who was presented to them in clear unmistakable terms, it turned out they did not love the truth.

We *must* love the truth! Love for truth is a gift from God that we must choose to receive by grace. In the last days, those who will not do so will perish. We would be well-advised to continually seek this grace, especially as we see deception abounding more and more.

"...that is, the one whose coming is in accord with the activity of Satan, with all power and signs and false wonders, and with all the deception of wickedness for those who perish, because *they did not receive the love of the truth so as to be saved.*" (2 Thess. 2:9,10, emphasis mine)

What is our response when God's truth is revealed to us, but it does not line up with *our interpretation* of the Bible? Do we embrace the truth or hold on to the tradition with which we have grown comfortable? God is bigger than any collection of biblical information about Him, and surprises await anyone who thinks they have Him figured out. Having love for the truth (a love for the ultimate reality of God's person and purpose) is a protection from being deceived in these tumultuous days of increasing darkness. Many voices are sounding forth in the land and new revelations are being proclaimed, but mixture abounds! If we do not have security in our knowledge of the Bible, where is it to be found? Very simply, in Him!

Educating our minds is not a solution for deception. Deception is primarily a matter of the heart, not of the mind. The greatest cause of deception is pride. A Christian can have his mind filled with sound theology and yet, in his heart, see himself as greater than he really is. If this is the case, he is already deceived (Gal. 6:3).

"I urge you therefore, brethren, by the mercies of God, to present your bodies a living and holy sacrifice, acceptable to God, which is your spiritual service of worship. And do not be conformed to this world, but *be transformed by the renewing of your mind,* that you may prove what the will of God is, that which is good and acceptable and perfect. For through the grace given to me I say to every man among you *not to think more*

*highly of himself than he ought to think;* but to think so
as to have sound judgment, as God has allotted to each
a measure of faith." (Rom. 12:1-3, emphasis mine)

Those who think more highly of themselves than they
ought (pride), will not have sound judgment in spiritual
matters. Spiritual perception will be clouded, and as a result
they can be led astray. However, God promises to renew the
minds of those who present themselves to Him in true
humility.

"God is opposed to the proud, but gives grace to the
humble. Humble yourselves, therefore, under the mighty
hand of God, that He may exalt you at the proper time."
(1 Pet. 5:5,6)

Pride is spiritually destructive. It prevents one from receiving grace from God and thereby brings opposition from
Him! However, when we humble ourselves at His throne, He
lavishes grace upon us. This is how we appropriate grace
for initial salvation, and it is also how we appropriate it to
*grow* in Him. Humility must become a life-style. Humility
guarantees more grace. When truth is revealed, we must
humble ourselves and receive it even when it is painful to
do so. Truth is more than just facts, for God speaks to reveal
*Himself.* As a result, we may recognize personal areas that
need adjustment, areas that are out of harmony with *Him.*
Yes, it may hurt! How do we receive a love for such discipline?
God gives grace to the humble. As we humble ourselves
before Him and present our need for grace, He responds in
love. The act of humbling ourselves does not make us
humble. It simply puts us in the position where God can

provide the grace needed to embrace His dealings as *He* works His character into us.

The gospel is the message of truth. It is more than good information and biblical facts. It is *God revealed through His word.* When preached, it brings the hearers face-to-face with God Himself. Our message concerns more than initial salvation; it is the *whole* counsel of God (Acts 5:20, 20:27). The *Church,* therefore, also needs to have the gospel preached to her. We who know God must continue to receive a love for His truth, if we would have sound judgment in the days that lie ahead.

# Chapter 21

# The Gospel

"In Him, you also, after listening to the message of truth, the gospel of your salvation—having also believed, you were sealed in Him with the Holy Spirit of promise." (Eph. 1:13)

"So faith comes from hearing, and hearing by the word of Christ." (Rom. 10:17)

Our salvation originated in God Himself. Just as He spoke and authored all creation, in like manner He brought us forth as *new* creatures in Christ. He spoke through the preaching of the gospel. We heard, responded in faith and were born of His Spirit. The spoken word of God is the most powerful force ever given among men! When God says something, whether directly (in an audible way or in that still small voice within our own hearts), through the Scriptures or through one of His servants, there is a performance of that word!

"For the Kingdom of God does not consist in words, but in power." (1 Cor. 4:20)

"For I am not ashamed of the gospel, for it is the power of God for salvation to everyone who believes." (Rom. 1:16)

The gospel we preach is not simply a collection of facts from the Bible, it is God declaring through us the truths recorded there. One can quote Bible verses to another all day long and accomplish nothing. However, when God *a-noints* the word, it has an impact with eternal consequences. This is not to belittle the study and memorization of Scripture. Such effort is necessary to communicate the gospel effectively; but, head knowledge of biblical data must not be confused with kingdom life. Depending only on education is one reason why preaching today has not produced New Testament results.

"And for this reason we also constantly thank God that when you received from us the word of God's message, you accepted it not as the word of men, but for what it really is, the word of God, which also performs its work in you who believe." (1 Thess. 2:13)

The Thessalonian believers recognized the difference between men speaking *about* God and God speaking *through* men. Because they *had* received (past tense) the gospel as God's word to them, it *was* performing (present tense) and would continue to perform (future tense) an eternal work in them. After Paul left Thessalonica, the gospel was still active and achieving God's purpose in their lives. The power of the gospel continues to operate long after the ones who spoke it have left the scene! The gospel is not just "dead letter." It is God, actively at work through His word, through people who function as His mouthpieces in the earth. It is thrilling to declare God's word in a situation and then watch the supernatural results that follow. Many times those results do not happen when *we* think they should or even *in the way* we think they should. However, God makes this promise to us:

> "For as the rain and the snow come down from heaven, and do not return there without watering the earth, and making it bear and sprout, and furnishing seed to the sower and bread to the eater; so shall My word be which goes forth from My mouth; it shall not return to Me empty, without accomplishing what I desire, and without succeeding in the matter for which I sent it." (Isa. 55:10,11)

God's word is His servant, and He entrusts it to the care of His people. As such it is one of the most sacred stewardships given by God (1 Cor. 4:1,2, Jas. 3:1). Since He sends His word to accomplish *His* desire, we who handle it must be very careful that *our* personal desires are not our goals when we speak it. The Bible says we are co-workers together with Him (1 Cor. 3:9). Thus, we are to have our hearts in harmony with His, so that our *labors* contribute to the working out of what His word was sent for! If we have impure motives (seeking recognition, wealth, power, prestige with men), God may still honor His word through us and accomplish much (people saved, healed, delivered). However, our efforts and ministry will be misdirected. Ministers have often confused God's honoring of His word through them as His approval of their lives, motives and overall direction of ministry. This is a grave mistake. God will honor His word, but He will also judge the motives of all men, especially those who speak for Him.

> "If any man's work which he has built upon it remains, he shall receive a reward. If any man's work is burned up, he shall suffer loss; but he himself shall be saved, yet so as through fire." (1 Cor. 3:14,15)

We choose how and what we build with upon the foundation of Jesus Christ. When the day of the Lord comes, He will test the quality (not the quantity) of every man's work. If we have produced a grandiose structure of straw, it will all be consumed. We will still be saved, though perhaps barely.

Our labors must be in harmony with God's purpose. As men have preached with unction from the Bible, there have been miracles wrought, powerful ministries established and the gospel proclaimed. Seeing this we have thought, "All we need is more of the same, and when *enough* has happened to satisfy God, Jesus will return." However, the day of fire is coming upon the earth, not to test the quantity as we see it, rather, the true *quality* of what has been done. Was *His* purpose accomplished in lives? The place to start is to determine to become as Paul, "a bond-servant of Christ Jesus...*set apart for the gospel of God."* (Rom. 1:1) Being set apart for the gospel is not synonymous with being in "full time ministry." It means our lives must be severed from the world system and given wholly to the Lord Jesus, whether we work at a secular job or not. (Paul often worked with his hands.) It means to be at God's disposal, to be in the right place at the right time, strategically located as His mouthpiece, so the power of God can go forth and set men free. We are literally to be set apart *for the sake of the gospel!* Then His word will not be twisted or hindered in any way as we share it with others. The *accurate* speaking of God's heart is crucial to the establishing of His purposes in our generation. If we walk with halfhearted commitment to Him and have mixture in our motives, He may still use us. He may still speak through us and His word may accomplish great things in the earth. We may even be thought of as "mighty in God." Nonetheless, we would be preaching a gospel of mixture. There will be elements of wood, hay and straw in that which we are building on the foundation of Jesus Christ. God desires that what we build *endures* in the day of the Lord, the day of fire. And endure it will, if we are a holy, pure people separated unto God for an accurate, anointed declaration of the gospel.

# Chapter 22

# Having Also Believed

"In Him, you also, after listening to the message of truth, the gospel of your salvation—having also believed, you were sealed in Him with the Holy Spirit of promise." (Eph. 1:13)

Even as every life form reproduces after its kind in the physical realm, so also God scatters His word as seed to bring forth a great harvest of spiritual fruit. He seeks fruit with the same nature as the seed He has sown. Even as apple seeds ultimately produce apples, so also the word of God brings forth children of God. Since we as His people are the channels for that word, we have a great responsibility to share it accurately. We are literally involved with the reproductive process of divine life!

"...for you have been born again not of seed which is perishable but imperishable, that is, through the living and abiding word of God. For, 'All flesh is like grass, and all its glory like the flower of grass, the grass withers, and the flower falls off, but the word of the Lord abides forever.' And this is the word which was preached to you." (1 Pet. 1:23-25)

In a cyclical sense, all flesh is like plant life. Even as grass dries up and flowers fall from their stems, so also the human body wears out and eventually dies. However, God's word is different; it is eternal. It is from this imperishable eternal word of God that we have been born. We are not simply flesh any longer. We are the product of the eternal Spirit and the word of God. The new birth is a miracle every time it occurs! The minute one hears and believes God's word with faith, he changes species! He becomes a *new* creature. Obviously our bodies remain flesh, yet, believers are no longer simply *of flesh*, they are *of God!* This new creation requires a life source from heaven. Jesus said of His disciples,

"They are not of the world, even as I am not of the world." (Jn. 17:16)

Jesus came from heaven, and through Him that is where our citizenship lies. *We are a people of heaven, living on the earth!*

The problem that arises, however, is to get our thoughts and actions to line up with the reality of what God has done in our spirits. God wants the miracle that has taken place in our lives to *become visible* in practical ways.

"Therefore, putting aside all malice and all guile and hypocrisy and envy and all slander, like newborn babes, long for the pure milk of the word, that by it you may grow in respect to salvation." (1 Pet. 2:1,2)

We must put away all the attitudes from our old lives that no longer fit our new identities. One may be sixty years old in the natural, but if he has just come to know the Lord, he is a spiritual babe. We need to hunger for God's word in the same way a baby longs for milk. An infant does not have to be persuaded to drink milk. He cries in order to get it! Such a desire is equally crucial for us as God's people, in order to grow in respect to our salvation. Sitting under teaching alone is not enough for spiritual growth. Rather, we must *hunger* for His word just like that infant longs for milk. With *this* kind of hunger, we *will* grow in our salvation, even as a baby grows in the natural.

If we fail to see ourselves as babes and rely on our natural abilities to analyze, examine and evaluate, we will bring forth flesh in the Kingdom of God. Since such abilities did not enable us to see God's kingdom in the first place (He had to reveal it to us, Jn. 3:3), why should we rely on them now?

"That which is born of the flesh is flesh, and that which is born of the Spirit is spirit." (Jn. 3:6)

When there is a mixture of the flesh and the Spirit, the stench of the former will soon become evident. For example, carnal judgment will display harsh criticism, malice and slander. In doing this, one may appear very sophisticated and express well thought out opinions on the issues and yet contribute nothing in an eternal sense to the purposes of God. This occurs whenever one does not see himself as a babe who desperately needs the pure milk of the word.

Another characteristic of a baby is its helplessness. When sincere believers grasp their total inability to comprehend the Kingdom of God apart from revelation, they will *long* for the milk of the word. They know that if revelation does not come, they will never understand how to walk before Him. They long for *insight* into this strange realm of the Spirit where they have been catapulted. It is like a whole new world that needs exploring.

There is always a danger, however, of losing our sense of helplessness once we begin to acquire greater knowledge concerning the things of God. It was not when He was a babe lying in a manger that Jesus said He could do nothing apart from His Father (Jn. 5:19), but when He was the fully mature Son of God, standing in His role as the Messiah of Israel and manifesting the character of God! Jesus never lost this sense of dependency on His Father. However, we often do, because we tend to rely more on *what we know* than on He Who has revealed it to us. This leads to pride instead of humility. In Peter's epistle, he wrote to Christians, *some of whom were mature elders in the church.* He said in effect, "In your heart attitudes toward the word of God, *all of you, both young and old,* become like babes who long for milk so that you may grow." When Christians lose this hunger, they need to be filled again with the Holy Spirit.

Faith can be literally born in people's hearts when they hear God speak to them. Ministers must not simply impart knowledge, but reveal Christ Himself who is the Truth! To accomplish this, our hearts *must* be filled with the One sent from heaven to reveal Christ. The Kingdom of God is properly presented whenever the one who speaks for Him recognizes his own personal spiritual poverty. When one seeks a word from the Lord, *knowing he has nothing to minister apart from revelation*, then God will delight in speaking to him. As that individual is then faithful to deliver the word, a supernatural extension of the Kingdom of God occurs to those who receive it in faith. Therefore, our call is to humility and brokenness before God. To such people He gladly reveals His truth and authority. Apart from Him, we can do nothing. By His grace we will seek only the increase of *His* government, *His* kingdom and *His* glory. In doing this we will seek nothing for ourselves.

# Chapter 23

# Sealed in Him

"In Him, you also, after listening to the message of truth, the gospel of your salvation—having also believed, you were sealed in Him with the Holy Spirit of promise." (Eph. 1:13)

If a dispute arises in society over a piece of property, ownership can be proven through a title deed. Similarly, when there arises a question concerning a particular business contract, a man's signature on the document testifies that the words written on it express his will. In biblical times, a man's *seal* declared his ownership and was considered equal to his signature. God also endorses this principle. Since the beginning of time, there has been an unseen struggle over the souls of men. However, *God has sealed those who belong to Him with the Holy Spirit.* By doing so, He has declared His ownership both to them and to the whole spiritual realm, including satan and the angels. His people often describe themselves as Baptist, Catholic, Protestant, Charismatic, Fundamentalist, non-denominational and on and on. They seek to find their identities in such descriptive words, and they can tell who belongs where by looking at the "labels." However, God looks only for His seal. In seeing it, He knows those who are His.

No matter how much shaking comes upon the Church, no matter how many men fall into deception and ungodly practices, and though we see the faith of some faltering, the foundation of God in the earth has been sealed with this ultimate truth: *He knows those who are His!* In Timothy's day, deception and ungodliness had spread in the Church like an infection. Nonetheless, Paul's counsel to him was heartening.

> "But avoid worldly and empty chatter, for it will lead to further ungodliness, and their talk will spread like gangrene. Among them are Hymenaeus and Philetus, men who have gone astray from the truth saying that the resurrection has already taken place, and thus they upset the faith of some. Nevertheless, the firm foundation of God stands, having this seal, 'The Lord knows those who are His,' and, 'Let everyone who names the name of the Lord abstain from wickedness.' " (2 Tim. 2:16-19)

When one turns from the truth and goes into error, perhaps even deceiving others, God is not taken by surprise. He fully knows what is in the hearts of all men. However, when such things happen, *we* need to be encouraged that He is still ruling and His purposes are not being thwarted. In the midst of shaking, we can have faith that we will not "get lost in the shuffle" because the Scriptures assure us that we have been sealed by God. He clearly sees the seal He has imprinted on our hearts. The true condition of the Church may confuse some as deception abounds and false prophets proliferate. However, there is no confusion in heaven. His insight is perfect. He knows those who are His.

There is yet another side to this equation.

"Let everyone who names the name of the Lord abstain from wickedness." (2 Tim. 2:19)

God's part is to recognize His seal, whereas our part is to abstain from wickedness and live for Him. Here is truth in tension. On one hand we see the divine sovereign knowledge of God and, on the other hand, we recognize our responsibility to obey Him. Some Christians focus more on the sovereignty of God; others focus more on human responsibility. Scripture teaches both emphases. Some would say that if God already knows those who are His, we might as well live any way we want. After all, what difference does it make? God already knows what will happen. For these people, the second part of the verse is very appropriate. Others would say, "Well, with all the deception going on in the earth and the shaking in some fellowships, does God really have a handle on what's occurring?" Their faith is weakened by what is happening around them. These folks need to be reminded of the first half of the verse, that the Lord knows those who are His, including *them!*

No matter what may occur that would suggest God's plans are in jeopardy, we can be solidly established on the foundation of God's sovereignty in the lives of His people. If you are His, He is not going to be deceived about it! There has been a seal applied to your life that He never loses sight of. At issue then for us who know Him, is not whether we have been sealed, but are we *reflecting His ownership* of us.

"Now in a large house there are not only gold and silver vessels, but also vessels of wood and of earthenware, and some to honor and some to dishonor. Therefore, if a man cleanses himself from these things, he will be a vessel for honor, sanctified, useful to the Master, prepared for every good work." (2 Tim. 2:20,21)

One can be sealed by the Holy Spirit and become a vessel for honor that is useful to the Master. One can also be sealed and become a vessel for dishonor, not at all useful to the Lord. Once we see our position in Him, will we live in such a way as to reflect it? The seal on our lives is obvious to Him. *How obvious is it to those around us?* We are to be clearly identified as His. One practical implication of this is how we relate to a local church. Do we identify more with the labels of men or with the seal and ownership of God? Are we known more by the emphasis of the Christian group(s) or organizations to which we belong or by our relationship with Him? *He* has us related to a particular group, but the group does not give us identity. It simply defines that part of the sphere in which the Master has placed us. We are children of *God* participating in *His* strategy, as we function in a particular part of *His* vineyard. Therefore, we stand as a testimony of *His* ownership in that part of *His* Church. We must not be swayed by the thinking of those who confuse their identity with a particular denomination or organization. "Come join us," they say. "We are the true people of God. Don't be joined to that other group. They are not as spiritual as we are." Such talk comes from a competitive spirit. To think in that manner is to not understand God's seal on His people. It is a mind-set that seeks to define those who are His and comes from a lack of confidence in God's seal and of His insight into the hearts of men.

God's strategy for His Church is greater than man's plan to gather and organize believers. Our efforts at labeling believers only brings *premature corporate identification* as to what is His and what is not, and divides God's heritage. If we create a group of Christians with our seals on them, they will be identified with us. We may then appear successful, because of the number who use our label; however, God's heart will be grieved. To take the seal of man and place it over the seal of God only brings confusion. Another sect is added to the already cluttered spiritual landscape. The world does not need more people saying they are the "true people" of God or the "most spiritual" or the ones with all the answers. May God help us to understand what it means to be sealed by the Holy Spirit of promise. May we see ourselves as one *part* of the whole, all of which is *His* and not be sectarian. May we not build people unto ourselves but unto Him. May we not seek only excellence in our ministries and spheres of influence, but rather that we contribute to the growth of *His* inheritance.

# Chapter 24

# Sealed in Him
# With the Holy Spirit

"In Him, you also, after listening to the message of truth, the gospel of your salvation—having also believed, you were sealed in Him with the Holy Spirit of promise." (Eph. 1:13)

We have been purchased by the blood of Jesus; we are His possession. Furthermore, He has declared His ownership of us by imprinting His seal into our hearts through the Holy Spirit. In addition to marking ownership, there is another purpose for seals. They testify to authenticity.

"He must increase, but I must decrease. He who comes from above is above all, he who is of the earth is from the earth and speaks of the earth. He who comes from heaven is above all. What He has seen and heard, of that He bears witness; and no man receives His witness. He who has received His witness has *set his seal to this, that God is true.*" (Jn. 3:30-33, emphasis mine)

In the midst of all that is counterfeit, all that falsely offers hope and fulfillment to mankind, there is one authentic Savior of men. He is Jesus the Christ. Scripture calls us to set our seal to the fact that God is true. We do that by believing His word and receiving His Son. By our lives, actions and faith, we testify to what God has done and is doing in the earth. We declare it to be a fact that Jesus was sent from the Father.

> "...I write so that you may know how one ought to conduct himself in the household of God, which is the church of the living God, *the pillar and support of the truth*." (1 Tim. 3:15, emphasis mine)

Today many reject God, and their lives and actions declare His word to be false. In effect, they call Him a liar. However, there is a people who have placed their seal on what God has done. This act puts their lives and reputations on the line and they become permanently identified with the purposes of God. When one says something is authentic, he runs the risk of being in trouble if later it proves to be counterfeit. He laid his name on the line; he certified it, only to discover it was false.

God asks us to lay our lives on the line if we have found His word to be true and His character trustworthy. Satan would have us believe that God may fail us or is not committed to us. Satan seeks to undermine the character of God in our minds. If he can cause us to doubt God's character, then what can we have faith in? His word? What good is someone's word if their character is faulty? So the thought comes, "God may desert you! He may just walk away from you even though He said He never would. God can't be trusted!" Satan always attacks God's character. However, if God is trustworthy then His word is also true, even if every man is found to be a liar. Our foundation is solid because we are built on Him. This is the ultimate question every hearer of the gospel must face. Is God worthy to be trusted? Can I lay my whole life on the line for Him and what He has promised? Or will I be swayed by the enemy and begin to doubt when he says, "You are a fool to trust in God. He will let you down and leave you holding the bag. He will get you to put your seal to something, identify with it and say it is authentic. It will turn out to be a sham. You are going to look like a total fool!" If we believe satan's lies, we will hold back from total commitment to God and His purposes. This is exactly what the enemy wants. But God *is* true! He *is* worthy to be trusted! We *can* take our lives and place them into His hands. The end result will not be those who believed *God* looking like fools; the victims will be those who decided He could not be trusted.

*A foundation stone in a successful life is the belief that God can be trusted.* Life is to be the adventure of faith! As He leads us into circumstances we have never experienced, we can watch for His hand of intervention to enable us to succeed in what He sent us to accomplish. Christianity is not a dull regimen of rules and regulations. It is the revelation of Christ—not only in the Scriptures, but in real life situations of Christian experience. God may assign us tasks that are beyond our ability. If all we see is our own ability (or inability), we will hold back from what He has called us. However, if we are persuaded He can be trusted, and we understand that it is His intention to meet us and empower us to do His will, then it makes sense to step forth in faith.

As we set our seal to the fact that God is true, He will place His seal upon us, thus authenticating us as His people! He wants His possession to be clearly seen in the earth. However, satan acts to confuse the issue. The proliferation of all that is counterfeit (cults, eastern religions, the occult, humanism, and so forth) is simply satan's attempt to obscure what is genuine. If one places a hundred silk or plastic flowers around a real one, it is difficult to tell which one is authentic. How then do we identify the genuine? What is His seal?

"...you were sealed in Him *with the Holy Spirit of promise...*" (Eph 1:13, emphasis mine)

*He Himself, His presence,* is what marks us as unique among all the people of the earth. God intends to reveal what is authentic with an unmistakable clarity for all to see before the end of the age.

Until then, there will be many voices with mixture sounding forth, even in the Church of Jesus Christ, and there will be many "plastic flowers" (cults) *surrounding* her true testimony as well. Although the authentic people of God do not stand out today with the heavenly distinction that marked the early Church, we should not be discouraged. Jesus told a parable about wheat and tares (Matt. 13:24-30,37-43). The wheat typified God's people, the tares spoke of the wicked, and the field was the world. Jesus said when the wheat bore grain, *then the tares would become evident as simply being the weeds that they are* (Matt. 13:26). The distinction between wheat and tares is not always obvious. Tares keep promising to produce the "goods" (the grain). Many unbelievers say that with enough money, education, political activism, social programs, man will be able to produce peace, prosperity and utopia on earth. Some believe that science holds the hope for mankind. For others, the answers lie in psychology, transcendental meditation, socialism or capitalism. However, hidden among all the tares of the world, there is a people marked with the seal of heaven. At the end of the age they are going to bear abundant grain and be manifested visibly as God's sons! That which creation has longed for since Adam will be found springing up in their midst. There will be justice, true righteousness, peace and joy. This company will stand in marked contrast to the tares who will be exposed as unable to produce the "grain" in the time of harvest.

"For the anxious longing of the creation waits eagerly for the revealing of the sons of God." (Rom. 8:19)

God is going to reveal His authentic sons. This will probably be a gradual phenomenon; wheat does not bear its grain instantly, all in one day. It grows over a period of time. Many Christians are expecting God to accomplish in them in one day, what He desires to do in them in their lifetime! While it is true that at His second coming we *will* be like Jesus instantly (in the sense of receiving our glorified bodies), He wants to develop His character in us *now*. He wants the fruit that testifies of His life increasingly manifest in our lives.

"And so we have the prophetic word made more sure, to which you do well to pay attention as to a lamp shining in a dark place, until the day dawns and the morning star arises in your hearts." (2 Pet. 1:19)

The day of the Lord dawns in conjunction with the Morning Star arising in our hearts. He will arise *in* His people, preparing us as He comes *for* His people. The increase of His life, presence and character in us shall mark us as His sealed possession at the end of the age.

Are we looking forward eagerly to His appearing? This is good. Are we also looking with expectancy for Him to arise *in* His people? Is our prayer, "Lord, come quickly"? This, too, is good. However, let me suggest this prayer also be on our lips. "Lord Jesus, may the wheat increasingly bear grain in these days. Cause that which marks us as unique and different from the tares of the world to increase in us. Lord, arise in Zion! You have sealed us with Your Holy Spirit and it is obvious to You who the heavenly people are. Lord, make the distinction more obvious here in the earth. May the level of Your presence rise in our midst. May the authenticating mark that characterizes Your unique possession in the earth be more manifest, in Jesus' Name. Amen."

# Chapter 25

# A Pledge of Our Inheritance

"...the Holy Spirit of promise, who is given as a pledge of our inheritance, with a view to the redemption of God's own possession, to the praise of His glory." (Eph. 1:13,14)

We have tasted of the future! The Holy Spirit within us is the pledge or down payment of our full inheritance. Through His indwelling presence, we have partaken of "the powers of the age to come" (Heb. 6:5), and the wisdom we now speak is not of this present era (1 Cor. 2:6). God intends that we be an "outpost" of the age to come, living in marked contrast to the world today. However, only to the degree that we embrace His presence and walk in harmony with Him will His power and wisdom be manifest in our lives and ministries.

"For indeed Jews ask for signs, and Greeks search for wisdom; but we preach Christ crucified, to Jews a stumbling block, and to Gentiles foolishness, but to those who are the called, both Jews and Greeks, Christ the power of God and the wisdom of God." (1 Cor. 1:22-24)

When an unbeliever considers Calvary, he sees weakness, he sees foolishness. For what is more feeble, more foolish than for God to come in the flesh and allow His own creatures to crucify Him? What purpose could it possibly serve? How could the crucifixion of one man have a personal, lasting impact on all other men, even years after it occurred? Yet in God's wisdom, when men believe the gospel and are baptized, God immerses them into the death and resurrection of His Son. Just as He came out of the tomb in glory, so they come out of water empowered in Him to live a new life. By faith, they experience Calvary for themselves. People who are spiritually blind, sinful, without hope and without answers are made into new creatures! Jesus' death and resurrection which appeared weak and foolish proved to be God's all wise, all powerful answer to nullify sin and its effects. To this day the message of Christ crucified remains both a stumbling block to some and foolishness to others. However, to those who are called of God, it expresses both His power and wisdom.

"Because the foolishness of God is wiser than men, and the weakness of God is stronger than men." (1 Cor. 1:25)

What constitutes the weakness of God? Is the One who created the whole universe ever weak? No. He is perfect in power. However, He stepped into weakness in His incarnation, so that we who are weak could be made strong in

Him. Consider the awesome holy Creator lying in a manger, small enough to be cradled in the arms of a young peasant girl in Israel. How weak! Yet in fact, how *powerful!* From that day on, cracks began to appear in satan's kingdom! God's power had been released in a way that the enemy never expected, and it set in motion those events that will lead to his destruction.

If we desire to move in the power of God during our generation, "the weakness of God" must also characterize our lives. Scripture teaches us to love our enemies, pray for those who persecute us and bless those who curse us. The world says, "Stand up for your rights. What are you? A weakling?" We agree, thinking to ourselves, "I can't do that, it's a sign of weakness!" However, Jesus said that if we are to be sons of our Father in heaven, we must live as He did (Matt. 5:44,45). If we want to become mature sons, moving in the power of God, we must embrace the truth that the weakness of God is stronger than men. Humanism cries out that man is able to determine his own destiny; self-actualization is the answer! We are told that man has power within himself to bring forth peace and prosperity in the earth. That same mind-set can also be seen in the Church, when Christians measure their performance for God by self-initiated activities. God has not called us to do great things for Him. He has called us to enter into the works that He has prepared for us and which He will do through us (Eph. 2:10). If we fail to understand our frailty, we will put confidence in the flesh (our own ideas, plans and programs for extending the Kingdom of God). We must lay such things down as they do not impress the Lord.

"He does not delight in the strength of the horse; He does not take pleasure in the legs of a man." (Ps. 140:7)

We must become impressed with "the weakness of God." *It is far greater than anything we could come up with!* The power of eternity is manifested through those who know that there is no strength or wisdom in themselves apart from God's anointing. He who was the greatest in God's kingdom said that apart from His Father, He could do nothing. Is that a picture of weakness? No, for *the power of heaven backs up those who live that way.* The One who made the greatest impact for the Kingdom of God was the One who went to the lowest place. Jesus took the sin of the whole world upon Himself and became a curse for us. He humbled Himself and because of this has been exalted to the highest place of all. He is now the King of kings! That is the way of the Lord. He who humbles himself will be exalted. God frequently calls us to go to the lowly place and humble ourselves. Our flesh protests, "I'll be seen as weak." However, such humility is necessary if we are to serve the Lord. His kingdom is not extended through the strength of man. The "weakness of God" is our strength. We must identify with both the "weakness" and "foolishness" of God for *that is how He has determined to extend His kingdom in the earth!*

"For consider your calling, brethren, that there were not many wise according to the flesh, not many mighty, not many noble; but God has chosen the foolish things of the world to shame the wise, and God has chosen the weak things of the world to shame the things which are strong, and the base things of the world and the despised, God has chosen, the things that are not, *that He might nullify the things that are,* that no man should boast before God." (1 Cor. 1:26-29, emphasis mine)

The present world system, which stands in arrogance, declaring itself to be wise and strong apart from God, will one day be crushed under His feet. Every knee will bow and every tongue will confess that He is truly Lord of all creation. *He* is going to bring this age to an end through a people who know that apart from Him they can do nothing. *He* is going to arise in the weak, the base and the despised with mighty signs and wonders, bringing forth His wisdom to nullify the wisdom that presently exists. We will see a confrontation between the Kingdom of God and the systems of this world. Whenever God's people arise and move in the Spirit, there will always be opposition from the world. Why? When they move in the righteousness of God and in the power and wisdom of heaven, they automatically come into conflict with those who move in the spirit of the present age. It is an inevitable confrontation. However, believers who do not understand that *their* strength and wisdom is useless, will misunderstand the *kind* of conflict facing them. Our warfare is not against people. It is a spiritual war! Our weapons are not based on human strength. They are mighty through God for the accomplishing of His purposes! We are not endeavoring to establish an earthly kingdom. We are not trying to take over the governments of this world. Our call is to declare the truth of His kingdom which is *already established in the heavens over every king and ruler on earth.* Even if they do not know it, every ruler occupies his place of authority only because Jesus has decreed it! He is the King of kings!

Therefore, we must not simply react to the trends of this age. We are to hear what the Lord wants us to do and then move in the wisdom of God with humility. We must seek nothing for ourselves; only His glory and His kingdom are to be extended. As the Spirit of God arises within His people, He will give us the power and wisdom to manifest Christ to our generation. As we live in harmony with the Holy Spirit we will literally be tapping the power of the ages to come. Thus, we will bring the "flavor" of eternity to bear on this present age. The Church will be a prophetic people preparing the way for the King to come in judgment and establish His visible rule over the whole earth. The Spirit we have received is our present day guarantee of the Kingdom of God to come in its fullness. Let us be filled with His presence and faith for the days that lie ahead!

# Chapter 26

# The Redemption
# of God's Own Possession

"...the Holy Spirit of promise, who is given as a pledge of our inheritance, with a view to the redemption of God's own possession, to the praise of His glory." (Eph. 1:14)

The gift of the Holy Spirit is God's pledge or guarantee that we will one day realize our full inheritance. Of course, we *presently* have the joy of the Lord in our hearts because we have come to know Him. However, the *full* realization of the promises of God lies in the future and we eagerly await it.

"And not only this, but also we ourselves, having *the first fruits* of the Spirit, even we ourselves groan within ourselves, waiting eagerly for our adoption as sons, the redemption of our body." (Rom. 8:23, emphasis mine)

This "full harvest" that lies ahead is far greater than the "first fruits" we have received. Deep within us our spirits groan as we await "the redemption of our bodies." His *presence* which we have experienced in our hearts will then be manifest in our bodies! The *redemption* which we have known in our minds will then be evidenced as well. This is why Paul says that God gave the Holy Spirit as a pledge of our inheritance with a view to the redemption of His possession. This would appear to be a paradox. If we are His possession, then this means He has already redeemed us. However, there is a *fullness* to our redemption that we await and it is to that which the Spirit points.

The salvation we now know as a *spiritual* reality will one day come forth visibly, touching the *physical* creation as well. Sin has infected more than just the hearts of men; it has infected the whole natural order! All the universe groans under its bondage to decay and corruption. Metal rusts, buildings crumble, pollutants corrupt the air and water. Morally, emotionally, philosophically, man continues to decline. The creation groans because it is "out of tune" with its Creator. It waits for the glory of God to be seen in the full redemption of His sons. Only as man is restored will the creation also be delivered from corruption.

> "For I consider that the sufferings of this present time are not worthy to be compared with the glory that is to be revealed to us. For the anxious longing of the creation waits eagerly for the revealing of the sons of God." (Rom. 8:18,19)

The sufferings we presently experience as we confront the issues and trials of this life, are nothing compared with the glory yet to be revealed *to* us and *in* us in that hour! For in that moment, the sudden visible manifestation of the glory in God's people will impact the earth bringing release from its slavery to decay. The first Adam introduced the decay; the last Adam removes it, and man will again rule over creation for the Lord (Heb. 2:5-8).

> "For the creation was subjected to futility, not of its own will, but because of Him who subjected it, in hope that the creation itself also will be set free from its slavery to corruption into the freedom of the glory of the children of God." (Rom. 8:20,21)

When God subjected the creation to frustration, He did so in hope. As its Creator, He also built that hope into the fiber of the natural order. All of creation has an inherent longing that anticipates the revealing of God's sons. Therefore, that which marks this age is an abiding hope and expectation of the glory of God! We who are believers look for that glory to be manifested within us! For creation, that manifestation is *its* way out of the existing futility.

The universe, marked by enslavement to corruption, hopes for the freedom found in the glory that the children of God presently taste. The Church today is to experience great freedom in a present measure of the glory of God in her midst. Freedom is to characterize the people of God. Not religion. Not law. But freedom! Freedom to serve, to worship, to obey and to be one with the Lord. Since we are the testimony of God's life and purposes in this age, we must learn to *live* in the glory of God. That is where freedom is found! Some may settle for commandments and theological philosophies.

However, when we learn to live in harmony with the glory of His life within us, we will find that the Christian life is marked by liberty. Jesus possessed total liberty to do His Father's will. Nothing held Him back. Too often, believers are restrained from moving wholeheartedly in the purposes of God because of weights and encumbrances that restrain and hinder them. This can take many forms such as pleasures of this life, precepts of man, constraints of traditions. However, in His presence there is fullness of joy and a freedom to live and minister as God always intended us to!

We must guard against living only according to what seems rational and logical. It is not that God is irrational or illogical. However, we do not comprehend nor apprehend the ways of the Spirit by relying on natural wisdom. We must learn to live by faith in an active communion with God. There He will reveal His wisdom and power to us. However, it is so easy to be pulled back out of that realm by the spirit of this age. Whenever God's people rely on intellectual reasoning or traditional methods, there is always a commensurate loss of freedom. A loss of freedom means that there is a diminishing of His glory in the midst of our assembling. Bond-servants of the Lord only seek to do that which they see their Father in heaven doing. The glory and presence of God abides with those who live in this manner (Jn. 14:23) and this brings freedom. A slave had no choice in being in servitude; a bond-servant was one who had freedom to choose servitude willingly (Ex. 21:1-6). It is in becoming *bond-servants* of the Lord that we experience true liberty. As we live in harmony with His Spirit, moving in *the freedom of obedience,* we become an example to all creation of that glorious liberty.

Today creation is enslaved to decay and corruption and cannot break free. However, a complete and final deliverance will come. The fact that we were created from the dust of the ground testifies of God's intention to liberate the rest of creation as well. By repenting from sin and a turning to the Lord, we enter that glory and freedom now. Creation however must continue to wait with an anxious longing for the full manifestation of the glory of God in His sons. Scripture portrays this as a travail similar to a mother about to give birth. Anxiety as well as yearning arise when the pains of labor signal the bringing forth of a new babe. Similarly, in creation there is an expectation of what is to come, but there is also travail, groaning and shaking within the creation as the future age approaches its time of delivery.

"For we know that the whole creation groans and suffers the pains of childbirth together until now." (Rom. 8:22)

At issue then is not simply the end of this present age. We are in a time of birth! As we view the turmoil and shakings in this present generation, both among people and in nature itself, it is not something to be feared. Rather, it is a time to celebrate! We are standing on the threshold of the age to come! Our day is about to arrive. We are not people of this age, but of the one to come. Let us then not be caught up in the spirit of this age, lest we be weak in faith when shaking occurs. Instead let us be filled with the Holy Spirit and bring the flavor of the future to bear on this generation. We rejoice to see that day approaching.

## Chapter 27

# Your Love for All the Saints

"For this reason I too, having heard of the faith in the Lord Jesus which exists among you, and your love for all the saints, do not cease giving thanks for you, while making mention of you in my prayers..." (Eph. 1:15,16)

Two traits of every Christian should be first, a vital faith in Jesus Christ and, secondly, a love for *all* of God's people. A sect usually views themselves as either the *whole* Church or, at least, the best, most mature, most spiritual *part* of the Church. Their mind-set goes something like this: "Hallelujah, if you want to be truly spiritual, you have to join our group. We are the most mature. We are the only ones on "the front lines" of what God is doing in this town."

However, such thinking reflects narrow vision with pride at the root of it. If in fact God does give a particular gathering of His people some insight on certain truths not found in other groups, what does He want them to do with it? They are to *serve* others with the fruit of that truth. If they sit with a sense of superiority, believing that they are more spiritual and more important, this evidences carnality, not spirituality. How easy it would have been for *God* to sit in heaven with a sense of smugness and superiority because of all He knew that mankind did not! Surely He is mightier than all the human race put together! Yet His desire is not to look down on men, but rather to find a way to *serve* and help them! Of course, this is what we also are supposed to do; *serve* others with the truth God has graciously given us.

Knowledge is not the mark of spiritual maturity. "Knowledge puffs up." (1 Cor. 8:1 NIV). *It makes one look greater than he really is!* When a balloon is blown up, it looks quite large until someone lets all the air out of it. Then its true size becomes obvious. God has to often deal with His children, to "pop our balloon," so we will see our *true* size! We are not as mighty in God as our knowledge leads us to believe! God wants reality in our relationship with Him. If we believe we have attained a certain level of maturity when in fact we have not, then there will be presumption in our hearts as we approach Him. We will assume God is impressed with our lives when in reality, He is offended by our attitude! It is dangerous to presume on God. Some have mistaken presumption for faith. They conclude that if they say or do a certain thing, God *has* to respond a particular way. However, God will not be manipulated by men, whether they quote Scripture or not! Scripture was not given so we could quote it and "call the shots" or control God "because He must act to confirm His word." If we stand in humility before Him, knowing Him as He *really* is and ourselves as we really are, we will express truth to others in a way that represents Him as a sovereign Being. *Truth ministered in humility will accurately reveal God; truth ministered in pride will only drive men from God.* Knowledge by itself (and this includes biblical knowledge) is not what constitutes the Kingdom of God; the Lord *Himself* is the essential content, the driving force of His kingdom. We must never be satisfied with knowledge alone. If we do not press in to know *Him* in an ever deeper way, then He will be missing from the emphasis of our speaking and ministry. We will be purveyors of knowledge more than revealers of God. If that were the case, would we extend the Kingdom of God through our lives? Being puffed up with knowledge, we would subtly (or not so subtly depending on how arrogant we are) gather to ourselves those who agreed with us. As a result of pride, we would drive from us those who otherwise could have been helped by the truth we possessed. Thus, God's kingdom would not be extended, but a sect would be established to create further division in the house of the Lord.

The major cause of division in the Church is not doctrine, but pride. Men substitute knowledge *about* God in the place *of* God. We allow ourselves to be puffed up through what we know instead of walking before Him in humility. Christian leadership especially will answer to God in this area.

"Let not many of you become teachers, my brethren, knowing that as such we shall incur a stricter judgment." (Jas. 3:1)

Whoever deliberately causes hurt and division in the Church, who draws men unto themselves while looking down in pride on others and criticizing those who see things differently, is in danger of severe judgment. Leaders especially must guard their tongues. What comes from one's mouth is but a reflection of what is in his heart.

"...For the mouth speaks out of that which fills the heart." (Matt. 12:34)

Men do not speak divisively simply because they do not know any better. They do so *because their hearts are not right before God!* He will not treat it lightly when men who claim they represent Him, in fact, actually misrepresent Him by seeking their own gain and prominence.

"If any man destroys the temple of God, God will destroy him, for the temple of God is holy, and that is what you are." (1 Cor. 3:17)

The context of this particular verse is that believers were divided over what leader to follow and identify with instead of being united as followers of Christ. Some were saying they were of Paul, others that they were of Apollos. In effect, Paul's response was this, "Listen my dear brethren, I planted the seeds of God's word in your midst. Apollos watered them; but God caused the growth! The one who plants or the one who waters is *nothing* in himself, *God* is the only source of supernatural growth!" (1 Cor. 3:4-7). If we understand this, then our gathering together will not be around gifted men (the *channels* of growth), but unto the One who *causes* the growth, the Lord Himself. When God's people gather unto Him, they will find others with the same motive. This is the key to true godly unity in the Church. Men cannot unify the Church! However, if our first emphasis was simply to gather together unto Him in true humility, endeavoring to serve one another, God would "fine tune" our hearts and bring a corporate harmony by blending our lives together. Sects form when people gather together around knowledge, interpretations of biblical truth, and (or) men who are capable and persuasive in speech. The way out of the present divided condition of the Church is for leadership to present the Lord before the people in His rightful place in *all* things. Programs, plans, committees and anointed men are not the key. They may be part of the process, but they are not a substitute for the Lord's presence. When we recognize and believe in Him as the true source of our life and growth, then, like the Ephesians, we will have first, faith in the Lord and, secondly, a love for *all* the saints.

A primary attribute of the Lord is His love for *all* His children. One attribute of fallen man is *selective* love. People love others because they are similar in personality or ministry or because they are of the same ethnic group or religious affiliation. However, when a redeemed people gather unto Him, opening their hearts to *Him*, He will reveal and deal with whatever is wrong in their hearts. He will do so because He is after purity and unity in their collective worship and life as a church. True unity is a miracle, but God is not content with anything less! Organizational unity is not sufficient.

God desires to reveal *Himself* with such clarity that the only response is to humble ourselves before Him. If we have faith that only He can bring us to maturity, the pressure will be off of us to accomplish it ourselves. *We will be free simply to serve others with truth because we love them.* The ultimate unity of Christ's body will come as His people give *all* of their hearts to Him. Then we will find how far short of His glory *we* are. Then there will be no room for pride as He sends us out to minister. We will go both as servants and learners, not as experts. God will get the glory because He is the One who causes the growth!

# Chapter 28

# A Spirit of Wisdom and of Revelation

"For this reason I too, having heard of the faith in the Lord Jesus which exists among you, and your love for all the saints, do not cease giving thanks for you, while making mention of you in my prayers; that the God of our Lord Jesus Christ, the Father of glory, may give to you a spirit of wisdom and of revelation in the knowledge of Him." (Eph. 1:15-17)

We need revelation from God, for without it, we have only head knowledge. Revelation must be at the heart of both individual and church vision and ministry.

"And as for you, the anointing which you received from Him abides in you, and you have no need for anyone to teach you; but as His anointing teaches you about all things, and is true and is not a lie, and just as it has taught you, you abide in Him." (1 Jn. 2:27)

This verse in no way negates the need for teachers. We need all of the five ministries Jesus has given to the Church to equip the saints for service (Eph. 4:11-13). However, it is not the teachings of men, but revelation from the Holy Spirit that we need. Church leaders are not custodians of a defined repository of knowledge that they dispense to the saints. They must hear from God! If those who feed the sheep are not *themselves* spending time in the presence of God, hearing His voice and sharing what He is revealing to them, the Church will be hindered instead of helped to grow in the knowledge of God. It will stagnate. Knowing God is a fresh, ongoing, daily experience. The minute one's ministry becomes stale, that person has stopped drinking from the river whose source is heaven. Nothing gets old there! The river of life that flows from God's throne is always fresh! The aging process in our physical bodies is the result of Adam's fall. We are *used* to growing old. But this should never occur in our walk with God, for this relationship was born from eternity!

"The Lord's lovingkindnesses indeed never cease, for His compassions never fail. *They are new every morning;* great is Thy faithfulness." (Lam. 3:22,23, emphasis mine)

The ongoing expression of God's mercy to the Church is a daily revelation of His character and love for us that never grows old! Our lives should reflect the freshness of the river of God, not a stale intellectualism where definition and information have been substituted for the water of life.

When dryness is experienced in a gathering, it is not because God has deserted His people. Rather, it is because they have lost their thirst for Him! Then, relying on natural talents, they come to *not expect* God's visitation in their midst. While meetings may be formally correct, something is radically wrong! The yardstick of spiritual orthodoxy is not a matter of the mind, but of the heart. Dryness in individual hearts is the *root cause* of dearth in the gatherings! If some would return to the Lord with all their hearts as *individuals,* they would find the river of life springing up within them and flowing out to others. These combined rivers would produce floods of fresh revelation of truth!

Of course, such a scenario makes many nervous. Why? When God starts moving in the midst of His people, things cannot remain as they were before! You cannot simply ignore God! Change must come! New courses of direction must be faced. However, any who have not fully responded to God will not appreciate what is occurring. Tensions and friction will arise in the camp! At this point, everybody faces decisions. Those now moving anew in God do not want to compromise what He is saying. On the other hand, others may be hearing truths they do not understand and simply do not know *what* action to take. What is the solution to this potentially explosive situation? They need God's Spirit of *wisdom,* as well as His revelation. So often when we see a new revelation, we fail to wait for God's wisdom concerning what to *do* with it. We tend to race forward with our new truth! After all, it is so obvious to us! Should we not just share it with everyone? We forget that what is so obvious to us now *was not* clear a short time ago! Consider the patience God had in bringing us to the point where we could even *hear* what was in His heart, much less be committed to *walk* in it. When we forget how long it took God to get through to us, we tend to be impatient with others who do not respond quickly. To extend God's kingdom, we must know how to handle the revelations He gives to us. For this, we need the wisdom of God.

To begin with, we need to know *His timing*. *When* does He want us to share? In speaking to His disciples, Jesus said,

> "I have many more things to say to you, but you cannot bear them now." (Jn. 16:12)

There was a vast amount of truth that Jesus wanted to share with His followers, but the Father's timing to speak had not yet come. Nor were the disciples ready to hear. However, when the day of Pentecost came, the Spirit of truth was poured into their midst and He began to reveal the heart of God to them. Even Jesus (who was truth personified) had to submit to the discipline of the Father as to *when* to reveal certain truths of the kingdom. Knowing truth, but not being released to share it, is a difficult discipline. If our desire is simply to show off what we know then there will be no qualms about speaking *whenever* we want to. On the other hand, if our desire is to reveal God, then His timing for speaking is absolutely essential. Our primary goal is not to expound what we know to others, but to do our Father's will.

A second factor in how to speak is one's *heart attitude*. We may possess truth and yet hurt people because we speak out of a wrong attitude such as malice, anger or jealousy. Jesus not only expressed accurately *what* the Father wanted Him to say, He spoke in such a way that He revealed the Father's heart!

"And I know that His commandment is eternal life; therefore the things I speak, I speak *just as* the Father has told Me." (Jn. 12:50, emphasis mine)

If judgment was the context of His words, that is what Jesus accurately conveyed. If it was a word of sorrow or compassion, He wept as He delivered it. Sometimes words of judgment caused Him to weep as well (Luke 19:41-46). In Jesus, we find not only the *truth* of God, but *wisdom* and truth in operation together. Jesus knew how to express the Father's heart. Thus when He spoke He could say that the Kingdom of God was in their midst.

A third and final factor in speaking is *with whom we are to share.* Correct timing and right heart attitudes are irrelevant if we address the wrong people! Jesus was sent specifically to the lost sheep of the house of Israel. Paul was sent as an apostle to the Gentiles. Peter, James and John, recognizing Paul's sphere, nevertheless saw themselves as sent to the Jews (Gal. 2:9). God's people are to know to whom they are sent and what their sphere of service is. The best of intentions will fail if we are not serving in the proper place.

May His Spirit of wisdom and revelation be poured upon us as we seek to know *when* and *to whom* we are to speak and may we do so with a *proper heart attitude.*

# Chapter 29

# The Hope of His Calling

"I pray that the eyes of your heart may be enlightened, so that you may know what is the hope of His calling, what are the riches of the glory of His inheritance in the saints." (Eph. 1:18)

When God called us to Himself, He did so with hope and expectation. Our sinful condition did not deter Him. In fact, it never crossed His mind that He might be involved in a futile effort. God's hope is not like man's; it is based on an eternal perspective. In contrast, our best hope in the natural is based on uncertainty. "Well, I *hope* everything is going to be all right." When God considers the Church in its present condition, He speaks with confidence concerning the future, for He has seen the "finished product." He comes to us in our time-space world and ministers to us from His perspective of seeing both the beginning and the end (Isa. 46:9-10). He pours His Spirit into our hearts to give us this eternal perspective! Thus, we can learn to see as he sees. We are not to think like the world; we have the mind of Christ! Our thoughts are to reflect His viewpoint.

Hope denotes a perspective bound by time. When one hopes for something, it is because he cannot see it yet. It will be fulfilled in the future.

> "For in hope we have been saved, but hope that is seen is not hope; for why does one also hope for what he sees? But if we hope for what we do not see, with perseverance we wait eagerly for it." (Rom. 8:24,25)

Hope concerns what is future. So how is it that God, who dwells in eternity, who has seen the future, has hope? Why should He even need hope?

One reason God identifies with hope is because *we need it,* and all our needs are met in Him. God knows that we are bound in time. Unless He comes and imparts hope to us, we can only face the future with uncertainty, even with fear and trepidation. From the foundation of the earth, God committed Himself to relate intimately with us. In order to experience not only our need for hope, but all of our needs, He who is limitless stepped down into the boundaries of our existence and tasted limitation! The Incarnation was God put into human terms; it placed Jesus within our constraints. Since He experienced our weaknesses and limitations, as our High Priest He ministers to us with true understanding and compassion.

> "Therefore, He had to be made like His brethren in all things, that He might become a merciful and faithful high priest in things pertaining to God, to make propitiation for the sins of the people. For since He Himself

was tempted in that which He has suffered, He is able to come to the aid of those who are tempted." (Heb. 2:17,18)

The Lord clearly understands every temptation that we face in the areas of doubt, fear, depression or hopelessness, because He was made like us. Therefore He is able to pray and intercede on our behalf with insight and effectiveness. He does not just sit in heaven and tell us to "pull ourselves up by our bootstraps" and try harder. No. He comes to us by His Spirit, ministering to us according to our need. If our problem is a lack of hope, then He ministers to us out of His own nature. He does not just *give* us hope; He *is* our hope!

"...Christ in you, the *hope* of glory." (Col. 1:27, emphasis mine)

Herein lies a mystery. Hope relates to what is *not yet seen*, and yet God who sees all is a God of hope! How precious it is that He is able to minister to us so effectively, meeting us in our limitations! He experiences the circumstances of our lives, identifying with us in them.

For example, God is patient. But how can He be patient if He already knows how everything is going to turn out? Out of His foreknowledge He has seen how His purposes are going to succeed, how long it will take and all the ingredients needed to accomplish them. From His eternal perspective it is already finished! So He can reign with confidence and peace because of His eternal viewpoint. Where then is the need for patience? Again, herein lies a mystery and also a great joy to all who believe. God *not only knows where we are going, He is going with us!* He is not just sitting at the end of the road waiting for us to arrive. He is on the road with us! Jesus is not only the goal of our faith; He is *the way!* God joins us on the journey!

Another mystery involves sin and righteousness. When we sin, He does not just casually view it from afar, unaffected by our wrongdoing because He knew we would stumble before the fact. He is *pained* by our sin; He *grieves* over us! How can God who foresaw it be so affected when we sin? Did He not see it from all eternity? Has He not already seen every sin we will yet commit? Does He not hold tomorrow as well as the past in His hands? Yes, He does. But God has stepped into vulnerability so that He can be both blessed and grieved by us. We would not have a genuine intimate relationship with Him if this were not so. He would just be like a great computer in the sky to which we could type a little prayer and receive some forgiveness whenever we needed it. Since He has chosen to participate with us in our walk and since it is a two-way relationship we have with Him, our actions greatly affect Him. What an incredible thought! God walking in the vulnerability of His people!

On this basis we can recognize how hope *must* also be part of His character. For God not only sees the future from eternity, *He looks toward the future from the present together with His people!* This is where hope comes in. I believe He is looking expectantly to the days and years that lie ahead for the Church! He is not sitting back with only an eternal perspective, indifferent about what is coming. His heart pounds with anticipation and excitement at what is on the horizon. A bride is being prepared for Him who will be without

"...spot, wrinkle or any such thing." (Eph. 5:27) As He considers her beauty (in spite of the amount of work yet to be done in her), *hope* fills His heart!

When the Scripture speaks of "the hope of His calling," it is referring to the hope in God's heart which He gives to us when He calls us to Himself. When we were called we did not have any hope. We were devoid of it and without Him in the world (Eph. 2:12). However, when the Lord touched our lives, He came with a plan for the future. He had something in mind, personally tailored and designed for each one of us. But what is the hope of His calling? What does He desire to bring forth in us and to minister through us in the years ahead? What has He seen from eternity that He longs to realize in our lives? The answers will be different for each of us. We do not all have the same ministry, giftings, place in His body or degree of visibility. But we do all have the same destination.

> "Therefore having been justified by faith, we have peace with God through our Lord Jesus Christ, through whom also we have obtained our introduction by faith into this grace in which we stand; and *we exult in hope of the glory of God*." (Rom. 5:1,2, emphasis mine)

We have tasted a measure of the glory of God and our appetites are whetted! We have partaken of something from eternity. We will never be the same again! Having touched the reality of God and having experienced Him for ourselves, we can never be satisfied with anything less than *He Himself!* Our desire is for more of *Him! He* is our destination!

What is the guarantee that we shall possess our inheritance, this laying hold of the glory of God in its fullness?

"Now faith is *the assurance* of things *hoped for,* the conviction of things not seen." (Heb. 11:1, emphasis mine)

Faith is the certainty within us that we will receive that for which we are expectantly waiting. Faith has come to us by the word of God, and thus we are assured of the glory of God. We exult in hope to see it realized, and we know that it will be ours!

## Chapter 30

# The Working of the Strength of His Might

"I pray that the eyes of your heart may be enlightened, so that you may know what is the hope of His calling, what are the riches of the glory of His inheritance in the saints, and what is the surpassing greatness of His power toward us who believe. These are in accordance with the working of the strength of His might which He brought about in Christ, when He raised Him from the dead, and seated Him at His right hand in the heavenly places, far above all rule and authority and power and dominion, and every name that is named, not only in this age, but also in the one to come." (Eph 1:18-21)

The Church today faces the same issues as the Ephesian Christians. Did God raise His Son from the grave and seat Him at His right hand in the heavens? Is Jesus far above all earthly and demonic authority? If so, then we have the same power in us today that was operative in raising Jesus from the dead! The power that established the throne upon which the King of kings reigns is the *present* power which brings about God's plans for *our* lives in *this* generation! God is actively fulfilling His purposes today, just as He was two thousand years ago.

Why is it so difficult for us to believe this? I suggest it is because we are intimidated by the age we live in. We see wars, genocide, political unrest, and are tempted to conclude that God is far away, uninvolved in it all. When we see famous and powerful men affecting the course of nations and thus the direction of history, we find ourselves pondering the question, "Is the King of kings really ruling behind the scenes over all that is happening?" It *seems* that the ones who influence the world the most are those who speak the *least* about God and His Son Jesus. The visibly *significant* ones of the earth tend to consider Christ to be insignificant as a source of help for the major problems facing mankind. So for the Church to claim that the person of Christ and men's relationship to Him is the most significant matter confronting the earth requires a real step of faith. It goes against the mind-set of this age!

However, God *has* called us to stand and go *with* the flow of heaven and *against* the forces here on ʌarth. He intends that we speak with authority of this King who reigns behind the scenes as supreme ruler of the universe! The enemy would make us believe we are irrelevant to the issues of this age. If we believe him, we will *mute* our voices when we should be *proclaiming* the word of the King! What Jesus declares about certain issues is more important than anything decided in the United Nations. What is on His heart is more important than front page news. Jesus is *the most relevant person* in the universe! The only people on the earth who have the authority to declare what is on His mind are the people in His Church! That makes us very relevant! The enemy has repeatedly attacked the Church's relevance, and as a result one of her tendencies has been to try and *become relevant* in herself. However, Scripture does not instruct the Church to try and be relevant to society.

Only when we see Him as He really is (the King of the universe) and ourselves as who we are in Him (His Spirit-filled subjects), can we live with confidence and impact the nations of the earth. In contrast, if we focus on becoming relevant to the nations, we will lose the sharpness of our prophetic voice to them. Many fall for this trick of the enemy. In reacting to his lies, we have tried to establish our relevance through social, political and religious activities to prove how important and necessary we are. We have examined our ministry to people's needs and have drawn from it a sense of identity and security. By this, a place of importance is established for us in society. However, it is not what we do either for men or for the Lord that makes us relevant. It is because of *who He is! He is the King of the universe* and *because we are His people,* we are relevant whether we know it or not! We must stop trying to become something in response to the enemy's lies and simply *rest* in what the Lord says both about Himself and us! The power of God *has* raised Jesus from the tomb. God has seated Him at His right hand in the heavens far above all who are of significance in the earth! The tomb is empty and the throne is occupied. This same power is now given to us who have faith in His name. We must believe this, or we will not successfully impact our generation!

We are not the salt of the earth by seeking to become what people think they need. Our effectiveness comes from being to people what God says we are! What God *says* we are is far more important than what men *think* we are or ought to be. We must understand God's view of the world and of His Church if we are to fulfill our mission. We must be more influenced from the heavens than from the news- papers, economists or politicians. True identity and function comes from seeing our heavenly source; we are from God. He is alive within us. To the extent we are influenced by men, we will fail to express Him or our true identity accurately. If we become a people marked by earthly thought and philosophy, we will see our relevance in what men think and say of us rather than what God has said. We desperately need *God's* perspective in these days. We need His prophetic voice in our midst to keep us on track. Without it, we become molded by the world even while we try to impact it! We do not have to prove anything to society. We do not have to defend God's Name. He is big enough to defend Himself and protect us in the process! We are simply to be His people, His possession *in full view of the world.* Then as others see the effects of God's presence in our lives and hear the truth concerning our love relationship with Him, many will be persuaded to choose the Kingdom of God.

As long as our priority is to be something to the world rather than something in the Lord, our impact on society will be limited. We must face the question. Who is our Lord? Jesus or the needs of men? If the need of man is our primary motivation for serving others, we will eventually find ourselves overwhelmed with the magnitude of the task! There is an incredible amount of needs, both natural and spiritual. However, Jesus said His yoke was easy and His burden light. The immensity of man's need is not our burden to bear; *Jesus* is on the throne! The government rests on *His* shoulders, not ours. We do not "call the shots" concerning our service, *He* does! *He had and has a plan concerning all of man's need.* That plan includes Calvary. It also included being exalted to the highest place of authority in the universe and then commissioning His people as ambassadors to represent Him on earth!

The issue is not what we are doing to address the needs of man, but do we reflect His kingship and authority. Are we implementing His plan? Or are we doing what *seems relevant* and doing it in our own strength? That will never extend God's kingdom. We might appear to have a successful ministry and meet the needs of many. But God is extending His *kingdom* in the earth. The power of God is available to us who believe, not to do what seems best, but what He says; for that is best!

# Chapter 31

# Head Over All Things
# to the Church

"I pray that the eyes of your heart may be enlightened, so that you may know what is the hope of His calling, what are the riches of the glory of His inheritance in the saints, and what is the surpassing greatness of His power toward us who believe. These are in accordance with the working of the strength of His might which He brought about in Christ, when He raised Him from the dead, and seated Him at His right hand in the heavenly places, far above all rule and authority and power and dominion, and every name that is named, not only in this age, but also in the one to come. And He put all things in subjection under His feet, and gave Him as head over all things to the church, which is His body, the fulness of Him who fills all in all." (Eph. 1:18-23)

Jesus presently reigns as King far above all creatures on earth and in the spirit world as well. Not only is His name above all names *today*, but it *will remain* that way in the age to come, until He has put all His enemies under His feet. He now has and will continue to have all authority. This mighty King is ruler over the universe, and He rules in a unique way. He who was God manifest in the flesh is now joined spiritually to those who make up His body on earth. It is not an organization; together they constitute a spiritual *organism.* Members are alive, being joined in spirit not only with each other, but with Him who gives them life. They are the body of which He is the head. Neither is complete without the other. The body of Christ is a whole entity with an identity greater than its individual parts. What an incredible thought! The Lord who is far above all, who is the supreme ruler of the universe, has stepped into a relationship with a company of people, where He is *part* of them! Jesus not only functions as Lord of lords and King of kings, but as one part of His body, contributing to the whole, giving it direction, identity and cohesiveness.

Today, the task of the Church is to demonstrate and to proclaim Jesus' Lordship to the world, yet *we have undermined that message by our failure to recognize His headship in the Church!* When Jesus was exalted as King, the Father *then* gave Him to be head over all things to His body. Thus, Jesus' ministry as head of the Church is established on the basis of His kingship. Therefore, the Church ought to be characterized first of all by a willing obedience to His will. To not obey Him is to not recognize His authority. Of course, the Church has always declared that Jesus is Lord and King. However, while it is easy to talk of His lordship, it is something else to walk under it! Many say they are obeying God.

How can you disagree with them unless they are doing something obviously sinful? However, if God's people were truly walking in His will, His body would not be so divided. If it is true that all who *say* they are walking in obedience *really are* doing His will, if the Church indeed has the mind of Christ, then His thoughts must be scattered! Thus, the current lack of visible love and cooperation in the Church depicts Jesus as not having a sound mind! He has been portrayed as incompetent, a failure as head of His body. How often have two or more declared they have heard from God on the same issue and yet received different input and come to different conclusions? As a result, they then divide from each other with hard feelings, all in the name of doing God's will while still testifying to His lordship and headship! No wonder unbelievers often do not respect or reverence God. We have misrepresented Him in the earth; and we have done it under the guise of spirituality!

Jesus' ministry as head of His body is based on the established fact of His lordship. Therefore, if in fact we did walk in submission to His authority (lordship), there would emerge a true expression of His headship (a corporate, unified, cohesive people moving with the mind of Christ). His lordship, walked out in people's lives, will bring forth a united company, speaking with one voice out of a single heart to express His burden. It is foolish to justify our divisions and still proclaim that Jesus is Lord and head of His body! It undermines the very message we proclaim. We must repent for our failure to hear and obey Him as we should. We must repent for portraying Him as the cause of our present condition.

Jesus' lordship will not be visibly manifested to the nations till it is *first* established and walked out among His people. One initial evidence that we are truly walking under His authority will be a recognition of our need for all of our brothers and sisters in other Christian bodies. No local church or fellowship of churches is self sufficient, having no need for the rest of the body. We need each other. Together we must come to one mind. A unified strategy on the earth will reflect the mind of Christ in heaven. A unified action on the earth will fulfill the purpose that God has planned in heaven. A unified body of God's people will proclaim the oneness that exists in God. Jesus prayed:

> "...that they may all be one; even as Thou, Father, art in Me, and I in thee, that they also may be in us; *that* the world *may* believe that Thou didst send Me." (Jn. 17:21, emphasis mine)

Our unity is a key to the world's believing the gospel we preach! In effect Jesus said, "Father, I pray that all who believe on Me may walk together with such a oneness on the earth that it reflects the oneness I have with You. Father, this *must* happen so that the world *may* believe!"

God has determined to have a people on the earth whose life and ministry so reflect the reality of heaven that they impact the world. He has a plan to bring this about. His body is the fulness of Him who fills all in all (Eph. 1:23). However, for this to be so in practice, the Church must attain to the stature that *belongs* to the fulness of Christ (Eph. 4:13). In other words, we must attain to a corporate maturity in character, vision and unity that accurately completes on the earth He who is the head, reigning in heaven! Certainly, the Church has not yet attained to this. We have fallen so far short. We are divided over many petty things. Ambitious men seek to establish a name for themselves. Trust is not evident even between ministries with the same goal. Competition abounds. However, God has a plan! His prayer in the seventeenth chapter of John will be answered!

> "He who descended is Himself also He who ascended far above all the heavens, that He might fill all things. And He gave some as apostles, and some as prophets, and some as evangelists, and some as pastors and teachers, for the equipping of the saints for the work of service, to the building up of the body of Christ; until we all attain to the unity of the faith, and of the knowledge of the Son of God, *to a mature man, to the measure of the stature which belongs to the fulness of Christ.*" (Eph. 4:10-13, emphasis mine)

Some claim there are no longer apostles and prophets in the Church. This is not true. Scripture says that Jesus gave these ministries to the Church *until* we attain to the unity of the faith and to the stature of maturity that belongs to the fulness of Christ. Today the Lord is raising up these two ministries along with evangelists, pastors and teachers. He is giving them insight into His plan and anointing them to lay foundations in local churches so that His prayer might be answered. He will have a full grown, many-membered, corporate man standing on the earth, moving in the mind of Christ. The world will see and marvel. In that day, there will be no excuse for not believing that the Father sent the Son to die for their sins. Let us lift up our hearts in thankfulness for His great love and mercy toward us. Let us give ourselves to Him and participate in His plan as He brings this age to an end.

**The Diakonate** by Dale Rumble. This book has made a significant contribution to the understanding of God's people on the subject of *building the Church*. By carefully presenting the Bible's clear but much-neglected revelation on this subject, the author has allowed his manuscript to be lifted well above the category of "just another book" and into the very mainstream of God's great purpose in the earth. TPB-288 p. ISBN 0-906330-06-8 Retail $5.95

**Crucible of the Future** by Dale Rumble. Here is an incredible look into the 1990's by a former IBM futurist. In this book, the author turns his attention to the world of the future as it relates to the Church's triumphant but costly role in the last generation of this age. The Church will face the most challenging test ever of her devotion to the Lord, her purity and her real supernatural power. It is a glorious picture of restoration in the mist of international turmoil. TPB-168 p. ISBN 0-914903-89-6 Retail $6.96